PRAISE FOR

A SPOONFUL OF GRATITUDE

"As a psychologist who works with people on maximizing their potential for happiness, I am thrilled for readers to experience Najma's invaluable insights to help us enjoy life to the fullest. A comprehensive compilation of scientifically sound self-help advice, *A Spoonful of Gratitude* provides a reminder to us all of the ways that we can become the best versions of ourselves in simple and incremental ways. I couldn't be more grateful for Najma's contribution to the literary world of self-help."

SOPHIA GODKIN, PhD, Health Psychologist; Happiness and Relationship Coach, and Author of *The 5-Minute Gratitude Journal: Give Thanks, Practice Positivity, Find Joy*

"This is a gem of a book that you'll read over and over again. The book itself has short chapters filled with scientifically proven ways to use gratitude to change your attitude and your overall life. This book will really get you thinking and change the way you view things. Najma reminds you that it takes effort and intentionality to choose gratitude, but when you do, there are so many benefits. If you want a shift in perspective on how you view life and want to live it with more joy, happiness, and optimism, *A Spoonful of Gratitude* is a must-read."

SCOTT COLBY, Founder, Say It With Gratitude; Keynote Speaker; Author of *The Grateful Entrepreneur*

"*A Spoonful of Gratitude* is packed with powerful, practical, and research-driven strategies on using the power of gratitude to enhance your quality of life—both personally and professionally. Use these tips to reduce your stress and anxiety, boost your confidence, and take your self-improvement to the next level."

DEAN BOKHARI, Motivational Speaker, Podcaster, Author of *The Daily Gratitude Journal for Men*

"This book reads like a bowl of soup in which you find a lot of inspiration one spoonful at a time. It is good to see that gratitude plays an important role in this book, but that it doesn't present gratitude as the only thing that can help to have a more pleasant life. Self-confidence, optimism, and many other personal characteristics are addressed as important in a joyful and stressless life."

DR. LILIAN JANS-BEKEN, Founder, The Thriving Human Science Center

"*A Spoonful of Gratitude* is a collection of thoughtful, as well as scholarly, articles. One of the things that I have always enjoyed about Najma's writing is her blend of research and practical insights for application. From the time that I got acquainted with her as a guest on a podcast that I used to host, I have found Najma's work to be engaging and approachable for anyone and incredibly well-documented with research for those who are interested in going deeper. In her book, she includes a great compendium of work on gratitude with an amazing toolkit for living and working in the spirit of your best self."

DARIN HOLLINGSWORTH, Chief Gratitude & Accountability Officer, Odonata Coaching & Consulting; Former Host, *Working Gratitude*

www.mascotbooks.com

A SPOONFUL OF GRATITUDE

The articles in this book originally appeared, sometimes in slightly different form, in the following publications: *Psychology Today, The Huffington Post, Success Magazine, Entrepreneur Magazine, Mindful.org,* and *GratCircle.com.*

For more information, please contact:
Mascot Books
620 Herndon Parkway, Suite 320
Herndon, VA 20170
info@mascotbooks.com

Library of Congress Control Number: 2021917962

CPSIA Code: PRV1021A
ISBN-13: 978-1-63755-000-7

Printed in the United States

"You've taken a popular topic that has dominated coffee mugs, T-shirts, and tweets and turned it into a thoroughly researched, well-documented, highly organized, practical, and readable book. I am so excited to buy copies and distribute it to friends. *A Spoonful of Gratitude* is a darn good book. Thank you!!!"

NANCY LUBLIN, Founder, Crisis Text Line

"Whether you're already a believer in the benefits of a grateful frame of mind or not, *A Spoonful of Gratitude* will skyrocket your interest in being more grateful and give you practical tips so you can live life to the fullest."

STEVE FORAN, Founder, Gratitude at Work

"This book is filled with impactful and science-backed ways to use gratitude in your daily life. You can easily flip to any page for inspiration on how to better yourself."

KERRY WEKELO, Award-Winning author of *Culture Infusion: 9 Principles to Create and Maintain a Thriving Organizational Culture*; Chief Operating Officer, Actualize Consulting

"Gratitude endows us with resilience and joy. Embracing and cultivating this innate gift enables us to move beyond being a spectator of life to more fully and meaningfully participating in life. *A Spoonful of Gratitude: Tips to Reduce Stress and Enjoy Life to the Fullest* helps us understand why Marcus Tullius Cicero, one of ancient Rome's greatest philosophers, considered gratitude to be not only the greatest of virtues but also the parent of all other virtues."

DR. PAUL J. MILLS, Professor, Public Health and Family Medicine; Director, Center of Excellence for Research and Training in Integrative Health, University of California, San Diego

TO MY SISTER HOMA, MY BROTHER ABAAS, AND TO MY PARENTS.

A SPOONFUL OF GRATITUDE

Tips to **Reduce Stress** and **Enjoy Life** to the Fullest

NAJMA KHORRAMI, MPH

CONTENTS

PART IV: ESTABLISHING CAREER PATHS AND GOAL-SETTING

PART V: RELATIONSHIPS

PART VI: HEALING

PART VII: "ALL GOOD THINGS"

INTRODUCTION

It's easy to think things won't get any better, especially if circumstances feel tough. Your hopes and dreams might feel unattainable. If your circumstances are okay or good, you'll likely be fixated on making those circumstances (where you are in life) even better. Wherever you may be in life, this book can help you get to a better stage with more knowledge, purpose, and gratitude. The truth is: I wish I had known what's in this book when I was younger. And I know the tips work, because I have used them.

Yes, you *can* make things better, and this book gives you the tips, lists, and strategies to help you do just that. The ability to harness your inner unbridled potential—what you know that's inside you that hasn't fully blossomed—is within your grasp. If you are ready to feel motivated, inspired, or healed, herein is content that will help you get started. If you are ready to lead a healthy life infused with well-being, self-care, and reduced stress, herein is material to help you get started. If you are ready to understand how daily gratitude can lead to daily bliss, and repeatedly so, the content is here in this book.

As a public health professional, I wouldn't have been able to write this book without first choosing to develop my writing skills in my twenties. When I was a young child, my teachers praised my writing; I even wrote a short column for the community newspaper in middle school. After college, I didn't further develop my writing skills until graduate school when working on my master's. Eventually, I chose to write about exercise and self-help for a small, online publication in 2014. It wasn't until I was allowed to write for *The Huffington Post* and other mainstream platforms that this skill I chose to harness was on display for others around the world to read. I continue to develop and grow as a writer every day. This book is a collection of articles from the several platforms I've written for, and I hope you, as the reader, learn what I wish I had known all these years. It's never too late to learn and grow.

The book is organized into seven parts: the first is on gratitude, and the remaining six are on topics of self-help. There are seven parts total, with the self-help content divided into six subsections. Each article can be a stand-alone read (like in the *Chicken Soup for the Soul* series) for you to come back to any time you prefer for motivation and inspiration.

Finally, this book is intended to inspire acts of kindness—paying it forward—and a life enriched with gratitude. The material is meant to pave the way for good times, happy times, and celebrations. While tremendous hard work and dedication are prerequisites to satisfied living, there is no doubt the tips, lists, and strategies will help you get there by harnessing your talents and strengths like I did. The material is intended to keep you focused, resilient, and tough in this life you have chosen, but that has also been given to you. You are the star. Go shine.

PART I

GRATITUDE

3 WAYS GRATITUDE CAN BOOST YOUR SATISFACTION

Are you searching to reach the next phase in life—a new job, a new house, a life partner, starting a family? Certainly, we all have that list of things we hope to get or have. As life passes by, the road we are on, however, will not look exactly like a friend's path or a close relative's path.

We ought to recognize how each of our paths is uniquely blessed. In turn, how can appreciation of our blessings increase satisfaction? Let's see how gratitude can boost your satisfaction.

1. GRATITUDE CAN REMIND YOU OF THE POSITIVE ASPECTS IN YOUR LIFE.

Have loved ones in your life? Keep them close. Have a good relationship with yourself? Cherish the self-love. Are you able to donate your money, time, or other goods? Learn to appreciate the blessing of being able to give to others. Each of us might be able to use a reminder of what's going well for us when we don't feel satisfied or happy, or when that next opportunity seemingly passes by. Too soon we forget the positives in our lives. Hopefully, with the right amount of reflection, we can recall those positive aspects.

2. GRATITUDE PUTS THINGS IN PERSPECTIVE.

If things are difficult, being grateful makes difficulty feel seemingly less. Sure you might be blue, but look at all the wonderful things that happened to you! Perhaps you got a compliment, made someone laugh or smile, got recognition for your work, or were able to get a good night's sleep. No matter the difficulty, such wonderful moments happen to us, and we may not even realize it. Reminding ourselves of how the ups outweigh the downs to our day can help put things in perspective. Try writing your grateful thoughts down if you think that will help boost your mood or outlook.

3. GRATITUDE CAN MAKE US FORGET OUR CONCERNS AND WORRIES.

When we actively treasure positive life moments, there's less time or room in our minds for other negative feelings. Sadness, frustration, or difficulty can become trivial. While working hard each day is important in spite of whatever difficulty, being grateful for our strengths and abilities can make our professional jobs or social lives seem less of an uphill battle and more of a blessing in disguise.

Practicing gratitude daily or frequently is key, however, to lasting satisfaction. In turn, a positive and satisfied attitude can help smooth the bumps of lost jobs, tough relationships, financial strain, or other difficulties that we may encounter.

So, with the right amount of regular gratitude, satisfaction can fall in the palm of your hands. Discussing with friends and family who care about your well-being can be a great start to figuring out those blessings! Count them and remember that great things come to those who wait.

(*The Huffington Post*, June 2016)

4 MAJOR BENEFITS TO BEING GRATEFUL ON THANKSGIVING AND BEYOND

If you have on your "to-do list" to be grateful this Thanksgiving, it's likely, if you express gratitude beyond the holiday and into your routine, that you will benefit your overall happiness and unintentionally promote positive actions from others. How? There are at least four major benefits to being grateful, all of which can promote positivity and optimism, strengthen relationships, and help you pay it forward.

Here are the four major benefits to being grateful.

1. ROUTINELY PRACTICING GRATITUDE HELPS US EXPERIENCE INCREASED POSITIVE EMOTIONS INCLUDING INTEREST, EXCITEMENT, JOY, AND PRIDE.[1]

Gratitude increases dopamine and serotonin levels in the brain,[2] which are key neurotransmitters that give us feelings of contentment.[3] If we are grateful more often, the happiness-producing neural pathways strengthen, just as exercise strengthens the body. Neuroscience researcher Alex Korb, Ph.D., wrote in his 2016 book *The Upward Spiral* that in fact, by focusing on the positive aspects in your life, a grateful person "...increases serotonin production in the anterior cingulate cortex."[4] Possibly as stimulating as Prozac, expressing gratitude can help the anterior cingulate cortex regulate emotions, which is one of its central functions.[5]

2. GRATITUDE PROMOTES OPTIMISM, WHICH LEADS TO GREATER WELL-BEING.

Researchers from the University of California, Davis and the University of Miami found that after regularly expressing gratitude for ten weeks, study participants reported feeling more optimistic about their lives.[6] As a result, these participants exercised more and visited the doctor less often.

Optimism, in turn, has been shown to be a life-lengthening trait, based on a recent Harvard University study.[7] "The most optimistic women had a 16% lower risk of dying from cancer; 38% lower risk of dying from heart disease; 39% lower risk of dying from stroke; 38% lower risk of dying from respiratory disease; and 52% lower risk of dying from infection," according to the study.

In addition, there are previously researched mental health benefits to optimism, boosted, in part, by gratitude.[8] "Optimism may significantly influence mental and physical well-being by the promotion of a healthy lifestyle as well as by adaptive behaviors and cognitive responses, associated with greater flexibility, problem-solving capacity and a more efficient elaboration of negative information," write researchers in *Clinical Practice and Epidemiology in Mental Health.*

Overall well-being seems to be influenced by optimism, which gives us another reason to be grateful more often.

3. EXPRESSING GRATITUDE STRENGTHENS RELATIONSHIPS.

Robert Emmons, Ph.D., a gratitude researcher, writes, "When you become truly aware of the value of your friends and family members, you are likely to treat them better, perhaps producing an 'upward spiral,' a sort of positive feedback loop, in which strong relationships give you something to be grateful for, and in turn fortifying those very same relationships."[9]

Healthy relationships, consequently, make us happy. How? According to the longest-running study on human development by Harvard University,[10] the leading predictor of health and happiness in a person's life is the quality of their relationships. The cascading benefits of gratitude do not end with increased positive emotions or increased optimism: they include strengthening our relationships.

4. IF YOU RECEIVE GRATITUDE, YOU'RE MORE LIKELY TO PAY IT FORWARD.

If gratitude promotes benevolence, wouldn't that make for a better world? Consider this: Expressing gratitude to a loved one or friend can lead them to pay it forward. Receiving appreciation makes us feel loved—feelings that can inspire us to initiate more positive and helpful actions toward others. As positive psychology researcher Sonja Lyubomirsky, Ph.D., wrote in her book *The How of Happiness: A New Approach to Getting the Life You Want*, "Grateful people are more likely to help others [because] you become aware of kind and caring acts and feel compelled to reciprocate."[11]

Expressing gratitude promotes our happiness and paves the way for good actions. There's no better way to lift ourselves and bring joy this Thanksgiving than by being grateful as often as we can.

(*The Huffington Post*, November 2017)

THE POSITIVE IMPACT OF GRATITUDE ON MENTAL HEALTH

As a Crisis Text Line volunteer, it's clear to me that mental health is suffering in this country. Without exploring all the different factors that go into the worsening mental health condition, there is one thing we can do: Use gratitude to pull ourselves up. Gratitude has a positive effect on the brain that is linked to life satisfaction and improved well-being.

On the contrary, some researchers conclude that gratitude "can't fix everything," and has a limited ability to alleviate anxiety and depression.[12] In a study from Ohio University, Cregg and researchers analyzed twenty-seven studies with 3,675 participants. Researchers noted the studies included two regular gratitude interventions: 1) a "Three Good Things" exercise in which participants list three things which they're grateful for each day to reflect on; and, 2) a "gratitude visit" in which the participant writes and reads a thank-you letter to someone they're grateful for. Cregg and his team found that these gratitude interventions' impact on anxiety and depressive symptoms was "relatively modest" ($p < 0.01$) and may be attributable to "placebo effects."[13]

Meanwhile, several studies have concluded there are multiple benefits to gratitude which has also been supported by neuroscientific evidence. In 2019, Chinese researchers found the first neural basis linking gratitude to life satisfaction, in a study published in the journal *Emotion*.[14] In the study, the structural makeup of a region in the brain called the medial prefrontal cortex (MPFC), which plays a role as the "social hub" of the brain, was influenced by how grateful the studied participants were, eventually determining their levels of life satisfaction. Interestingly, the MPFC is also involved in human feelings of empathy and social decision-making. While prior studies show a correlation between gratitude and life satisfaction, the 2019 study is beginning to establish the neuroscientific connection between the two.

While neuroscience continues to explore the benefits of gratitude and positive psychology, there are several proven ways in which gratitude has a positive impact on mental health.

Here are at least five ways that gratitude improves our mental health.

1. GRATITUDE HELPS US FEEL VALUED.

Just like having a job makes us feel useful and valued, gratitude plays a role in making us feel valued in our lives. The recognition, which may seem rather ordinary, actually can boost self-esteem and self-value in ways not yet completely understood. Similar to how learning and achieving make us feel good about ourselves, receiving or even expressing gratitude makes us each also feel valued and, in turn, improves self-esteem and self-value.[15] The results include decreases in anxiety, depression, and stress, and increases in self-worth, motivation, productivity, achievement, and more.

2. GRATITUDE MINIMIZES NEGATIVE HABITS, PATTERNS OF THINKING, AND FEELINGS.

When we focus more on the positive, we focus less on the negative. The results are more joy, satisfaction, appreciation, kindness, generosity, and empathy; and more positive expressions and behaviors. Gratitude, especially when expressed as a habit, helps minimize negative habits, patterns of thinking, and feelings, which often are the causes of depression, panic, and fear.

Expressing gratitude has the tendency to accumulate positive thoughts, which, similar to how light can pour through a window, helps wash away concerns, worries, and self-doubt. These negative emotions often are the root causes of stress, much of which can be substantially abated with regular and abundant amounts of gratitude.

3. GRATITUDE HELPS US REKINDLE OUR INNER CHILDHOOD WONDER AND AWE.

Routine feelings of gratitude expressed for things like nature, love, and connection, for example, can help us rekindle our inner childhood senses of wonder and awe. Louie Schwartzberg, an American time-lapse cinematographer, producer, and director, discusses in his 2011 TED Talk how gratitude can bring us to appreciate each new day for being so unique.[16] In my perspective, this is as if each new day is like experiencing and viewing a new flower; a new wonder—in turn, rekindling our inner childhood senses.

While seemingly simple, if we did see each new day in this way, our ability to motivate ourselves might come easier, with less stress, and much stronger mental health. Such a perspective may not come easily, but if applied and maintained, it can truly help live a fulfilling and meaningful life.

4. GRATITUDE HELPS US FEEL INSPIRED, WHICH CAN HELP WITH MOTIVATION.

Feeling inspired often can motivate us to learn, grow, change, improve, or adapt to difficult challenges and circumstances. Gratitude has the ability to help us feel inspired, in turn, promoting such positive behaviors and adaptations. While studies continue to highlight gratitude's neuroscientific effects on the brain, previous research has shown gratitude can help develop motivation. In a study from the journal of *Motivation and Emotion,* a team of researchers led by Dr. Emmons looked at 700 middle school students (mean age = 11.74 years) and found that gratitude led to greater motivation as well as additional positive effects such as social integration.[17] "Motivation" was defined, in part, by students wanting to contribute to "people and society" as well as to a "unifying purpose in their life." Therefore, it is true that gratitude has the ability to inspire and motivate, leading to positive behaviors and adaptations, providing key parts to a successful life rich with well-being.

5. GRATITUDE PREVENTS WORRY AND FRUSTRATION.

By allowing us to focus on what's good in the present, gratitude helps to prevent worry about the future. Frustration can dissipate as well. With the help of gratitude, we get less caught up with what a person says or does, instead focusing on the next good thing to help us move forward. It's kind of like a surfer always wanting to catch the next great wave. Stress and frustration cause routine feelings of anxiety, sadness, and depression, and if truly applied and worked on, gratitude can help mitigate such feelings.

The abundance of good from gratitude fuels an abundance of good in return. Of course, finding our passions, practicing self-care, exercising, genuinely expressing ourselves when possible, building strong relationships, eating well, and more are part of a fulfilling life recipe; however, gratitude is often where a successful life starts. The positive impact of gratitude on our mental health is undeniable. Hopefully, you've got a gratitude routine down pat or are considering starting one.

(*Psychology Today*, June 2020)

WHY EXPRESSING GRATITUDE STRENGTHENS OUR RELATIONSHIPS

Do you have one person in your life whom you feel grateful for? Perhaps two or three persons? How often might you say "thank you" to them for what they do, or who they are? Expressing our appreciation for people we are grateful for can strengthen our relationships in deep, meaningful, and rewarding ways.

Research shows that expressing gratitude for those we care about can improve the relationship for both parties by bringing us closer to the other individual and sustaining the relationship for the long term.[18] If you need more convincing, here are five ways that relationships benefit by showing gratitude.

1. EXPRESSING GRATITUDE SHOWS YOU CARE.

When we show gratitude toward another in a relationship, we acknowledge a trait found in the other person. Psychologist Sara Algoe and researchers, in the first study demonstrating that gratitude strengthens relationships, writes, "Relationships with others who are responsive to our whole self—our likes and dislikes, our needs and preferences—can help us get through difficult times and flourish in good times."[19]

The expression of gratitude to another who shows responsiveness to our whole selves shows we care for the recipient of that gratitude. Expressing gratitude is a powerful way of displaying our affection, and in terms of our relationships, brings us closer together.

2. EXPRESSING GRATITUDE ACKNOWLEDGES A GOOD DEED BY THE OTHER PERSON.

Psychology professor Barbara L. Frederickson describes gratitude serving in part as a "moral barometer." In her book, *The Psychology of Gratitude,* she goes on to explain that gratitude "provides a reading of the moral significance of a situation," and the recipient of said gratitude acknowledges benefiting from a "moral action."

Put another way, when we say "thank you" to another, we often respond with appreciation for this good deed. Our appreciative acknowledgement reveals an exchange of give and take. By serving as this "moral barometer," gratitude allows the two sides of the relationship to initiate or respond to goodness, which ultimately deepens the relationship, making it more meaningful to both parties.

3. EXPRESSING GRATITUDE RECIPROCATES THE KINDNESS SHARED AND FELT IN YOUR RELATIONSHIP.

In addition to serving as a response to a good deed, expressing gratitude reciprocates kindness in our relationships. There is plenty to be said about kindness, too. After former NBA basketball star Kobe

Bryant died in a tragic helicopter accident, scores of acquaintances hailed the player's kindness off the court. Bryant's example makes it clear how sharing in feelings of kindness in our relationships really matters to both sides. So, why not share your appreciation for the individuals in your relationships? It can generate the kindness you might be missing.

4. EXPRESSING GRATITUDE CELEBRATES THE POSITIVE IN YOUR RELATIONSHIP, BRINGING BOTH SIDES CLOSER TOGETHER.

When our relationships might be missing kindness or the muster we're looking for, gratitude can be a starting point to discovering the positive aspects of our connections. Celebration of good moments—perhaps via an uplifting social media post or a handwritten thank-you note—can help bring both sides closer together. When left unexpressed, our gratitude won't pay off in our relationships and eventually towards our well-being, despite the fact that we care deeply for this well-being.

5. EXPRESSING GRATITUDE MAKES US FEEL HAPPY AND SATISFIED, AND PAVES THE WAY FOR FUTURE ACTS OF KINDNESS IN THE RELATIONSHIP.

Robert Waldinger's seventy-five-year study on adult development describes how our relationships are the biggest predictor of happiness and health.[20] So, if gratitude can strengthen our relationships, then why not combine both potent ingredients (quality relationships and gratitude) toward gaining a more satisfying life? In fact, just considering the gratefulness we feel towards others daily can be a strong start to strengthening our relationships, optimism, and mental health.[21]

By making us feel happy, satisfied, and encouraging the act of "paying it forward," gratitude strengthens our relationships and our lives on many levels.

Through strengthened relationships, we find greater meaning, depth in affection, and overall joy from the littlest of things—a compliment, a gesture; to the biggest of things—our overall satisfaction, optimism, attitude, and approach to living day-in and day-out. Let your gratitude for those you care about be the beginning of wonderful things to come.

(*Psychology Today*, June 2020)

GRATITUDE HELPS MINIMIZE FEELINGS OF STRESS

Gratitude is a strong strategy to help minimize stress in our lives, which is especially intense these days with coronavirus here to stay. Whether you are experiencing higher stress levels due to life events, your role as a caregiver, because you're searching for a job, or just as a pandemic survivor, evidence shows that gratitude can help you.

Here are at least three ways that gratitude helps minimize stress in our lives.

1. GRATITUDE LOWERS STRESS HORMONES IN THE BODY.

When a sudden stressful event or circumstances arise, the body responds naturally by releasing adrenaline and cortisol. Cortisol is responsible for increases of glucose in the bloodstream to facilitate activity in the brain and repair of tissues. When stress persists and turns into chronic stress, cortisol and other hormones are active routinely, which can lead to:

- Anxiety
- Depression

- Digestive problems
- Headaches
- Heart disease
- Sleep problems
- Weight gain
- Memory and concentration impairment.[22]

The ability to cope with stress involves the use of coping strategies, which can include the following:

- Physical exercise (e.g., outdoor walks, stretching)
- Eating well, staying hydrated, and getting plenty of sleep
- Fostering supportive relationships
- Practicing self-awareness and facilitating self-care
- Daily gratitude exercises

If incorporated, gratitude has the potential to be a potent coping strategy. Gratitude helps lower cortisol levels in our bodies by about 23 percent, preventing the health problems that stress can lead to.[23] What does that mean? You can help avert the negative consequences of stress listed above, which millions routinely face, through a regular gratitude practice.

2. GRATITUDE HAS THE ABILITY TO MINIMIZE CAREGIVING STRESS.

In a Chinese study of familial caregivers of individuals with dementia, the findings showed the beneficial role that gratitude plays in minimizing distress among caregivers.[24] The findings led researchers to suggest incorporating gratitude into non-pharmacological interventions among caregivers feeling distress while caring for persons with dementia.

3. GRATITUDE ALSO HAS THE ABILITY TO MINIMIZE JOB-SEEKING STRESS.

In one study of Korean undergraduate students from 2019, those in the gratitude intervention condition demonstrated a decrease in job-seeking anxiety and perceived stress, as well as an increase in life satisfaction, mental well-being, and happiness.[25] The study was intended to see if gratitude could help young adults reduce stress associated with job-seeking. Undergraduate students participating in the gratitude intervention were able to find greater meaning in their lives which helped to reduce stress levels.

WHAT CAN YOU DO?

Including a daily gratitude exercise is a habit that can work very well in releasing and removing stress. Write what you're grateful for in a journal, in a helpful and handy app, or in a thank-you note. Acting on feelings of gratefulness will strengthen the effects of gratitude as well, especially if made to be routine. The ability to empower yourself through gratitude is a key to self-care, less stress, and lifelong well-being and satisfaction. Try and be sure to take full advantage of this practice while you can.

(*Psychology Today*, July 2020)

GRATITUDE HELPS CURB ANXIETY

Research shows gratitude is a strong way to reduce anxiety. Such effects are in addition to gratitude's ability to strengthen relationships, improve mental health, and minimize stress. In fact, researchers suggest that gratitude's effects may be long-lasting and especially positive.[26] Multiple studies use gratitude interventions as free, simple, and effective ways to protect against anxiety. Promotion of self-understanding, reducing unbeneficial self-talk, and reducing anxiety in youth are ways in which we can benefit.

We all experience a degree of anxiety in our lives. Practically no one is free from it. In fact, there are several ways we can use anxiety to our advantage.[27] What does anxiety feel like? There are many different ways we can each experience anxiety,[28] such as:

- Feeling nervous, restless or tense
- Having a sense of impending danger, panic, or doom
- Having trouble sleeping
- Experiencing gastrointestinal (GI) problems

Knowing when anxiety becomes unbearable is key to maintaining a higher quality of life. The signs for when to seek help for anxiety include:

- You feel like you're worrying too much and it's interfering with your work, relationships, or other parts of your life.
- Your fear, worry, or anxiety is upsetting to you and difficult to control.[29]

There are steps to take to prevent anxiety from interfering with your life. Such steps include physical exercise, getting plenty of sleep, good nutrition, a strong social support system, and also gratitude. How does gratitude work to protect against feelings of anxiety? There are at least three ways that gratitude helps.

1. GRATITUDE LETS YOU BETTER UNDERSTAND YOURSELF IN ORDER TO TAKE IT EASY.

When we get overly critical of ourselves, stress can ensue. Self-compassion, self-understanding, and taking it easy are ways in which we hope to act. With gratitude, this is possible. Researchers in an Italian study found that gratitude "is connected to a less critical, less punishing, and more compassionate relationship with the self."[30]

The Italian researchers conclude, "being grateful renders individuals more prone to show kindness, comprehension, support, and compassion toward themselves when setbacks and frustrations occur."

Based on their findings, it seems the art of knowing oneself and taking it easy may very well be linked to our gratefulness.

2. GRATITUDE HELPS REDUCE UNBENEFICIAL SELF-TALK.

When facing a setback, stress trigger, frustration, or persistent worry, there is a tendency to engage in unbeneficial self-talk or repetitive negative thinking (RNT) linked to increasingly higher levels of anxiety.

The good news is that gratitude has the potential to reduce such thinking, according to a 2019 German study.[31] Researchers showed a significant decrease in RNT via an app-based gratitude intervention lasting six weeks. Interestingly, in a 2020 study in *Alzheimer's & Dementia*, RNT was linked to increased risk for developing Alzheimer's disease. By protecting against RNT, gratitude may have the potential to reduce the risk of Alzheimer's disease as well.[32]

3. GRATITUDE HELPS REDUCE ANXIETY IN YOUTH.

In her doctoral thesis, Danielle Cripps describes the way that gratitude can help reduce anxiety in youth. She writes, "A school-based gratitude diary intervention could be an effective way to promote school belonging and reduce anxiety in a youth population."[33]

Students in the intervention group were asked to write three things they were grateful for each day. By encouraging gratitude at a young age—especially in teenage years—anxiety may be lessened. Reviewing the ways youth can benefit can have a positive impact on our society at large.

In all, gratitude has the ability to reduce anxiety in unique and noteworthy ways. Researchers support the use of gratitude interventions based on findings from multiple studies, while some others express caution to rely on gratitude alone to curb anxiety.[34] Nonetheless, the majority of the evidence suggests there is plenty to gain from gratitude, including aid in the struggle with anxiety.[35]

(*Psychology Today*, July 2020)

GRATITUDE PROMOTES WELL-BEING IN HARD TIMES AND GOOD TIMES

When going through hard times, or even in good times, a grateful perspective is key. According to Dr. Robert Emmons, a leading researcher on gratitude, "In the face of brokenness, gratitude has the power to heal. In the face of despair, gratitude has the power to bring hope. In other words, gratitude can help us cope with hard times." As a country, if we can face the novel coronavirus together, we can practice gratitude together as a nation.

A vision of gratitude is key to surviving *and thriving* day-in and day-out. Compare where we are now to a year ago. Traveling was easy. Going out was simple. Crowds were no issue. We can be grateful today for the opportunity to have loved ones in our lives, friends, others to count on; or, if nothing else, for the simple joys of walking and eating, which for most have not been affected.

Hard times call for gratitude.

But then why do we easily forget gratitude? According to Dr. Emmons, "When times are good, people take prosperity for granted and begin to believe that they are invulnerable."[36]

Perhaps when circumstances are near the status quo, or what we're used to, we feel invulnerable. Most of us realize times are not great due to coronavirus. However, until we are directly affected and moved beyond status quo circumstances, there might not be enough incentive for us to regularly show gratitude. Is that the best strategy? No.

Gratefulness at this time is like getting proper hydration during an extremely intense workout. It is vital.

With so many families strained due to kids being out of school or a lack of childcare, loss of a job, death of a loved one, or coping with any illness, gratefulness (and self-care) should be our rock.

A vision of gratefulness includes boosting yourself with gratitude and positivity. Secondarily, a vision of gratitude includes boosting others with the same.

A 2019 study on gratitude and self-compassion in the journal *Mindfulness* found that both of these facets of mindfulness enhance psychological well-being.[37] The Italian study looked at roughly five hundred respondents, first asking them whether they meditated or not. Measures of mindfulness, self-compassion, gratitude, and psychological well-being were determined in both groups, subsequently, using professional scales and questionnaires. The study results showed that those who practiced meditation displayed greater dispositional mindfulness, gratitude, and self-compassion. The study also found that gratitude specifically was "associated with positive relations with others, self-acceptance, environmental mastery, personal growth and purpose in life."

In another 2019 study from *The Journal of Positive Psychology*, researchers found that "gratitude is beneficially, although modestly, linked to social well-being, emotional well-being, and to a lesser extent psychological well-being."[38]

While research does say that gratitude is not a cure for illness, physical or mental, there are strong indicators that gratefulness provides life satisfaction, overall well-being and stronger mental health.

With the beneficial role that gratitude can play in our lives, we ought to engage in more of it. How?

Here are three ways to engage in a gratitude practice.

1. Pick out three different parts to each day that you can be grateful for and enjoy them. For example, you might appreciate the peacefulness of the sun rising in the morning. Or you might like the excitement of TV shows at night. Or you might like taking a shower at the beginning or end of your day and feeling refreshed afterward. Enjoy these parts to your fabulous day.
2. Choose two people you interact with each day that you are grateful for, and pick out at least one thing you appreciate about them. For example, you might appreciate the candor your client speaks with at work. Or you might appreciate the thoughtfulness your sibling adds to a discussion on an important topic. Enjoy and appreciate these parts to your personal or professional relationships.
3. Share an uplifting social media post with a friend or loved one. For example, you might post an uplifting quote about gratitude with your friends on social media. Or you might celebrate your mother's birthday with a loving and heartfelt status post on a friendly and uplifting app or platform. Enjoy and celebrate these moments.

Your vision of gratitude can be renewed and reinvigorated daily with all the joys that life can bring. *You just have to open your eyes to them.*

Even in hard times, as we are all facing together, gratitude can be used to help us thrive and celebrate what we do have. In turn, gratitude can facilitate strength, comfort, joy, and peace when at times these seem beyond our reach. Try your hand routinely and get the most out of the practice that you can.

(*Psychology Today*, August 2020)

DOES GRATITUDE HAVE THE ABILITY TO HEAL?

There are a range of experiences in life, some of which cannot be forgotten. Some moments are blissful; some, painstakingly difficult; and others, neutral.

Together, we currently face an extremely difficult time. In this article, I will review some of the evidence that a regular gratitude practice can help upgrade our experiences, shifting our outlook on and experiences in life to more satisfying ones, especially in times of difficulty.

In the *Journal of Clinical Psychology*, Dr. Robert Emmons and Dr. Robin Stern write that gratitude "may spontaneously catalyze healing processes," and that "relatively easy techniques can be included to increase gratitude alongside existing clinical interventions."[39] Further, in their conference paper, researchers Kimberly Glasgow et al. state that "Gratitude has been found to be psychologically protective," especially after natural and man-made disasters. Glasgow et al. conclude in their paper by saying, "Gratitude is an important factor in resilience and healing after disaster."[40]

Perhaps in this time of COVID when so many of us are looking to protect, heal, or stay strong, gratitude can come to our rescue.

How does the healing process even work, psychologically speaking? With or without coronavirus, we each have experienced mental and emotional ups and downs that healing could aid. Yes, there are connections between the brain and our immune system that may only begin to explain some of how that kind of healing works. Still, the neuroscience of psychological healing is complex enough to admit we don't have it all figured out. Indeed, trying to explain any neuroscience behind the entire "healing process" is somewhat daunting. However, some researchers have studied gratitude's specific effects on patients and their well-being.

How does gratitude work to support psychological healing? A 2019 study looking at the expression of gratitude among breast cancer patients gives some insight. The study looked at forty-two female breast cancer patients. Each patient in the intervention group wrote reasons they were grateful for daily for two weeks. The study found that listing reasons for feeling gratitude daily "led to higher levels of daily psychological functioning, greater perceived support, and greater use of adaptive coping strategies."[41] That means that gratitude helped women fighting breast cancer feel better in terms of self-esteem, optimism, acceptance of illness, and affect, feeling they have a stronger support system as well as feeling an increased ability to cope with change.

If gratitude can help provide support, is "psychologically protective," and may aid in the healing process, then there is all the more reason to share in a gratitude practice right now. Our collective health can benefit greatly, while our outlook on life can simultaneously brighten considerably.

(*Psychology Today*, August 2020)

GRATITUDE AND ITS IMPACT ON THE BRAIN AND BODY

Scientific studies reveal that the effects of gratitude on the brain and body are complex, but calming, mentally strengthening, and motivating. With the rise of positive psychology in the 2000s, the study of gratitude has tremendously expanded. Here is a look at three effects of gratitude on the brain and body based on recent, rigorous scientific analysis.

1. GRATITUDE DECREASES HEART RATE (LIKELY VIA THE NERVOUS SYSTEM).

In a gratitude intervention where participants were asked to picture their mother and tell her, in their mind, how much they love and appreciate her, researchers found that heart rate decreased significantly compared to the non-intervention group. In this 2017 study by Kyeong et al., the non-intervention group was asked to focus on a moment or person that made them angry. In comparing the gratitude versus "resentment" groups, researchers concluded, "[O]ur results suggest that gratitude intervention modulates heart rhythms in a way that enhances mental health."[42]

The scientific relationship between heart rate and gratitude may be due to gratitude's effect on the parasympathetic and/or sympathetic systems, as stated by researchers. The parasympathetic system is responsible for slowing the heart rate and digestion regulation, while the sympathetic system is responsible for boosting heart rate and alertness, and sending blood to the muscles. Researchers specifically looked into the different heart rate effects between people expressing gratitude versus those expressing resentment.

2. GRATITUDE STRENGTHENS THE EMOTION-RELATED ACTIVITY OF THE BRAIN.

In the 2017 Kyeong et al. study, the gratitude intervention was observed via functional Magnetic Resonance Imaging (fMRI) to strengthen the participants' ability to regulate emotions. In other words, those expressing gratitude were able to rethink/reframe a situation in a more positive light.

The activity of the amygdala—a region of the brain known for its role in processing emotions—was observed to be specifically impacted by the gratitude intervention. The amygdala is an almond-shaped piece of tissue located on the sides of our brain, otherwise known as the "temporal lobes," and it is part of the limbic system, which is responsible for processing emotions and memories. When practicing gratitude, the amygdala's activity under the limbic system seems to be positively impacted. The research suggests that gratitude might help store and build positive memories of what otherwise might have been considered painful or difficult in our past.

3. GRATITUDE ENHANCES THE MOTIVATION-RELATED ACTIVITY OF THE BRAIN.

In the 2017 Kyeong et al. study, a gratitude intervention was observed via fMRI to enhance participants' motivation as well. Here, specifically, researchers looked at the activity of the nucleus accumbens (NA) during a rested state. The NA is responsible for the cognitive processing of motivation, in part, and its activity may be affected in individuals with major depression.[43] When engaging in a regular gratitude practice, the NA in the brain may very well be positively impacted.

The 2017 Kyeong et al. study ultimately suggests future studies should look at long-term gratitude interventions and whether they have an even greater impact on the brain and body.

In summary, the ability for a gratitude practice to positively impact the brain and body is increasingly clear from a scientific viewpoint. To take advantage of the evidence, picking up a regular gratitude exercise is essential. Just like exercise is helpful to the entire body, gratitude is helpful to the mind.

(*Psychology Today*, September 2020)

ARE EMPATHY AND GRATITUDE LINKED TO EACH OTHER?

The word "empathy" was first described in neuroscientific literature by Dr. Paul MacLean in 1967.[44] The definition used then was, "the capacity to identify one's own feelings and needs with those of another person." Today, a second definition of empathy offered by the Oxford Dictionary is "the ability to understand and share the feelings of another." Since 1967, decades of research have offered various interpretations of what empathy entails as a trait among humans.

Can the precise meaning of empathy really be known? While philosophical debates may linger over empathy definitions, this article seeks to highlight the overlap in neuroscientific evidence between what part of the brain is impacted by both empathy and gratitude.

A 2018 article discussing empathy in *Current Opinion in Behavioral Sciences* shows there is a clear role played by the medial prefrontal cortex (MPFC) in emotional empathy and associated positive emotions. Such positive emotions include pride, joy, happiness, motivation, and wonder.[45]

A 2019 experiment discussing gratitude in the journal *Emotion* shows there is a clear role played by the MPFC as well, influenced by how grateful study participants were. This particular 2019 study established the neuroscientific connection between gratitude and life satisfaction, looking specifically at the MPFC region.[46]

There is clearly an overlap between the MPFC's activation role in both empathy and gratitude based on the above studies. The MPFC may be the neuroscientific connection between these very unique and rewarding feelings among humans.

The MPFC is part of the prefrontal cortex (PFC). What is the overall purpose of the PFC? Executive function. Executive function serves a person in fundamental ways, including decision-making (from small to big matters of importance), interpreting reality, planning of complex cognitive behavior, personality, expression, and moderating social behavior.

Located within the PFC, the MPFC could be the reservoir where gratitude and empathy serve to enrich our minds and in turn reward us with some of the most desirable feelings among humans—joy, satisfaction, feeling meaningfully connected, and more. Future studies might look into the neuroscientific links between other fundamental emotions—including love and hope—with gratitude.

What could this mean for you?

1. YOU COULD PRACTICE GRATITUDE TO INCREASE YOUR EMPATHY FOR OTHERS.

Many times people are criticized for lacking empathy or not having enough of it. But ways to cultivate empathy might not be as widely recognized. Perhaps one way to increase your empathy could be to engage in a daily or weekly gratitude practice. The result could be more meaningful relationships, an understanding of others' circumstances and emotions, and even resilience in your own life.

2. YOU COULD PRACTICE EMPATHY TO INCREASE YOUR ABILITY TO FEEL GRATEFUL.

If you're struggling to feel grateful, the effect might be vice-versa. You could volunteer at a local food pantry, or alternatively, for a mental health hotline or messaging platform. You could gain feelings of empathy that could strengthen your ability to feel grateful.

(*Psychology Today*, October 2020)

SELF-CARE AND GRATITUDE: HOW THEY GO HAND IN HAND

With coronavirus affecting the global population and societies at large, the debacle begs the question:

What are we doing to initiate, promote, and sustain self-care?

For many, the glass seems half-empty. With loved ones tragically passing, or loneliness seeping into our daily moods, or responsibilities of kids overtaking many parents' schedules, there is reason to consider gratitude in our daily regimen of self-care. Turning to gratitude can, in part, help us see the glass as half full.

Here are three ways gratitude promotes self-care.

1. GRATITUDE PROMOTES SELF-CARE VIA HEALTHIER LIVING.

A brief yet regular gratitude practice promises more benefits than may be expected. For example, college students who write about what they're grateful for weekly for ten weeks also exercise more than those who engage in other types of writing.[47] A gratitude practice promotes exercise, better nutrition, better sleep, and not smoking, among other things.

2. GRATITUDE PROMOTES SELF-CARE VIA SELFLESSNESS AND HUMILITY.

Self-care via gratitude holds benefits for social well-being as well. Among three hundred college students, those picked to write gratitude letters showed greater stimulation in the reward region of their brains when observing money given to charity. A regular gratitude practice, in turn, motivates us to seek kindness and generosity to reward our minds as well as to improve circumstances for others; the latter, improving the lives of others, makes us more selfless and humble.

3. GRATITUDE PROMOTES SELF-CARE VIA MEANINGFUL CONNECTION TO OTHERS.

Another benefit for social well-being was seen among adults and college students in the U.S. and Korea asked to perform two gratitude activities: remembering a grateful experience, or writing a gratitude letter. Other participants engaged in activities such as hiking or shopping. Of the two groups, participants exercising gratitude felt more connected to others. (Loneliness, which is rampant due to COVID lockdowns, for example, might be tackled via gratitude practices.) Feeling socially connected in the time of COVID could go a long way to promoting self-care as well as societal care.

Countries are addressing COVID health consequences, but what about the self-care and societal care that's needed as well? Using a gratitude practice can address the needs of members feeling unfairly affected by the pandemic as it is a low-cost, high-impact tool. Not only does gratitude help at this critical time, but gratitude is also useful to individuals and societies beyond times of public health crisis. Hopefully, we apply such a practice daily or weekly to reap its countless benefits.

What are some ways you can practice gratitude?

- Use your social media platforms—or, alternatively, a journal—to list what you are grateful for weekly. Try to keep this up for over six weeks.
- Say "thank you" in-person to someone you care about.
- Say "thank you" to yourself before you go to bed, recounting three things you appreciate about yourself.
- If possible, appreciate the love shown to you by others by showing it back in ways shown in the first two points above.

(*Psychology Today*, October 2020)

HAVE YOU EXPERIENCED A LIFE-CHANGING EVENT? BE GRATEFUL

Have you experienced a life event that you didn't expect at all? Perhaps a failed relationship, unexpected loss of a loved one, or traumatic illness? Almost all of us have expected things to work out one way, and been blindsided when they didn't. We may still be suffering from the consequences, but we can still pivot and be grateful.

Gratitude is an attitude that is in our control. While it may not come naturally to all, expressing gratitude can become a habit we practice and fuel what is called post-traumatic growth (PTG), or personal growth, in us. Finding the little things in life to be grateful for can heal our wounds, transform the experience of suffering into joy, and consistently put us on the path to life success. While many have heard of post-traumatic stress disorder (PTSD), not many of us have heard of PTG.

In a study of male and female spinal cord injury (SCI) survivors, the majority of survivors went on to be especially grateful for everyday life after their life-altering injury.[48] Further, survivors were grateful for family support, grateful for new opportunities, grateful for a positive sense of self, and grateful to God. More specifically, SCI survivors were grateful, for example, for "reading daily newspapers early in the morning," "sitting outside in the evening listening to and seeing the birds," and "being able to play with their grandchildren."

In terms of their view of self, SCI survivors felt that they became "actually better" people following their life-changing experience. When facing a major unpleasant event in our lives, this finding translates into the opportunities given to all of us to become "better" people. "Better," in part, can mean more resilient and appreciative as opposed to "materialistic," "insensitive," or "superficial." While it may feel devastating during grief, trauma, fear or stress, personal growth, or PTG, is being able to discover hidden strengths and capacities as a result of struggling and coping with various life challenges. It is possible to gain strength and move on.

SCI survivors also expressed gratitude for family support. More specifically, their experiences led them to recognize the "significance of their family and become more grateful for the presence and support of their family." If family is not the answer, you may have friends that feel like family and whom you trust. You can use them as support during your recovery.

SCI survivors are not the only ones who benefit from demonstrating gratitude in aspects of their lives. Those who've experienced heart disease or cancer also show increased gratitude for life and what they already have.[49] Indeed, life-changing events fuel a noteworthy growth in people that increases one of the healthiest emotions in people: gratitude.

What if you've experienced a failed relationship or unexpected loss of a loved one? Will there be lasting suffering and pain? It may take days, weeks, months or years, but you will get there. Researchers have, in simple terms, identified that one of the five themes of PTG is an appreciation of life. Growth and appreciation following a life-altering event or trauma seem to naturally ensue and can be symbiotic. While not everyone has the same circumstances or responds the same way to such events, the research implies there *is* hope even after the most unexpected or traumatic of events. Remember, you *will* get there.

What can you do to pivot after changes in your life and reap the benefits of gratitude (rather than possibly nothing at all)? Try engaging in a gratitude practice. You can begin to adopt a few of the habits below.

- Use your social media platforms—or, alternatively, a journal—to list what you are grateful for weekly. Note the little things, like having soap to wash your hands or having a heated home, if you are so fortunate. Try to keep this up for over six weeks.
- Say "thank you" in-person to someone who you care about and who supports you.
- Say "thank you" to yourself before you go to bed, recounting three things you appreciate about yourself. Include things like a caring nature, personal grit and strength, or a sense of humor.
- Reflect on how you have grown as a person, and express gratitude for two to three of those things. Include things like "becoming stronger" or "becoming wiser."

(*Psychology Today*, November 2020)

GRATITUDE FOR OUR LIVES THIS THANKSGIVING: REFLECTIONS ON GIVING THANKS FOR THE YEAR OF COVID

"Every inhalation of the breath prolongs life and every exhalation of it brings joy to the soul."
—13th-century scholar and poet, Saadi

COVID has brought wreckage to families and loved ones across the globe. However, in the face of hardship, our gratitude for all that we have is bright. The 13th-century scholar Saadi describes each breath as "blessings for our souls"—a blessing that feels especially dear in the time of COVID. Whether we are directly or indirectly impacted by COVID, being able to appreciate the blessing of each breath is within our capacity.

Gratitude helps us realize this capacity. It leaves us rich inside. Are you able to contemplate the blessing of each breath this Thanksgiving?

For the person who reaches eighty years of age, they will take approximately 672,768,000 breaths in a lifetime.[50] Multiply by two (for each inhale and exhale) and you get 1,345,536,000 total inhales and exhales altogether. Over 1.3 billion. Could any of us faithfully say "thank you" for each and every part of those breaths? In other words, could you say "thank you" for the inhale that "prolongs life" and the exhale that "brings joy to the soul?" In the words of Saadi, "Whose hand and tongue is capable to fulfill the obligations of thanks to Him?"

Being grateful for the life circumstances that we have this Thanksgiving may be challenging given the effects of the global pandemic, despite many of us having been vaccinated. Still, it is possible to do. Encouraging one another to bask in just a bit of gratitude for our lives will uplift our spirits this Thanksgiving.

What can you do this Thanksgiving to show your gratitude for being alive?

- Share a motivational quote (if you want, linked to gratitude) with a loved one.
- Share what you are grateful for on a free social media platform like the Gratitude Circle app.
- Pay it forward by smiling or giving a compliment to a stranger.

By giving thanks, there are many ways an individual benefits, including spiritually, mentally, physically, and socially. Gratitude, with regular practice, has the ability to change how we feel and how we see the environment around us. Some of the neuroscientific rewards include rethinking a situation to see it in a more positive light; strengthening motivation; and even decreasing heart rate, as mentioned before.

Being able to reflect on the value of life can be grounding and rewarding. The opportunity to do so should be practiced more than once each year during Thanksgiving. Grounding can help us accept the circumstances around us. Rewards can include the mental, emotional, social, and physical rewards of being grateful for life. Combined together, these reflections can bring purpose and a fresh outlook for the following year.

Undoubtedly, these have been hard times. If seeing a silver lining means sitting with each breath long enough to contemplate even an atom of its value, then we have found the reward of gratitude.

Happy Thanksgiving to all.

(*Psychology Today*, November 2020)

GRATITUDE IS A GATEWAY TO POSITIVE EMOTIONS

Does expressing gratitude regularly seem flaky, fuzzy, or overly altruistic?

At the same time, do you feel stuck, upset, or like you're constantly chasing joy and happiness?

Giving gratitude a chance could help you along your quest to better mood and health. The scientific research on gratitude shows that, when routinely practiced, feelings of gratefulness are accompanied by more positive emotions.

Here are three ways that gratitude is a gateway to positive emotions.

1. GRATITUDE HELPS YOUR BRAIN PROCESS OTHER POSITIVE EMOTIONS, INCLUDING JOY.

If you practice gratitude regularly for at least two to eight weeks, it is likely you will experience increased positive emotions, including interest, excitement, joy, and pride.[51]

Gratitude increases dopamine and serotonin levels in the brain,[52] which produce feelings of happiness.[53] By feeling grateful regularly, happiness-producing neural pathways strengthen.

The Greater Good Science Center at The University of California at Berkeley suggests gratitude-journaling for fifteen minutes, three times per week, for two weeks to see positive effects.[54] *Forbes* magazine contributor Janet Miller suggests it takes eight weeks for brain patterns to shift and induce positive effects.[55]

Taking the first step towards your goal of feeling better begins with making gratitude a regular practice, in whatever method you enjoy.

2. GRATITUDE HELPS PEOPLE SAVOR POSITIVE EXPERIENCES FOR A LONGER PERIOD OF TIME.

In a study from the *International Journal of Applied Positive Psychology*, researchers discuss how gratitude "maintains positive emotions resulting from a positive experience."[56] Put differently, these researchers conclude that gratitude is able to "maintain elevated levels of positive emotions," at least for the short term.

Participants were asked to write about a recent achievement (i.e., their "positive experience"). Then a gratitude intervention was employed, asking participants to list factors for which they were grateful that contributed to their achievement for fifteen minutes (i.e., the "gratitude intervention"). The study found that the gratitude intervention led to elevated positive emotions at a subsequent stage compared to those in the control group.

This 2019 study suggests that by expressing gratitude for a positive experience, you are able to savor it. The next time you want to continue feeling elated after a joyful experience, consider using gratitude.

3. GRATITUDE AND JOY FEED OFF EACH OTHER—OR, IN OTHER WORDS, ARE SYMBIOTIC.

A study in *The Journal of Positive Psychology* found that gratitude and joy work hand in hand. Researchers conclude there is "an intriguing upward spiral between gratitude and joy: as one cultivates the disposition for gratitude, this increases the frequency of experiences of joy, which in turn should foster the disposition of joy, thus increasing gratitude."[57]

Even though researchers measured trait (i.e., "dispositional") gratitude here, the correlation between gratitude and joy is clear, revealing a symbiotic relationship that could be replicated in all of us.

In sum, for those seeking to feel better—and feel better more often—gratitude might be the handiest tool in your toolbox. The upward spiral of positive emotions, including more prolonged states of positivity, is undoubtedly just one of the quite favorable effects of a regular gratitude practice.

(*Psychology Today*, December 2020)

WHAT IS THERE TO BE GRATEFUL FOR IN 2020?

With COVID's impact lingering, many have experienced fatigue, tragic loss, disheartened mood, and other overwhelming feelings. It has not been easy, and such difficult emotions ought to be acknowledged inside ourselves. In fact, as part of the World Health Organization's strategy to address pandemic fatigue, public health experts collectively state we must "acknowledge and address the hardship people experience, and the profound impact the pandemic has had on their lives."[58]

Importantly, it is now in the thick of things that gratitude can lift our spirits or connect us to the present moments that we can still appreciate. Leading gratitude researcher Dr. Emmons describes a positive response to hardship when he says, "crisis can make us more grateful—but research says gratitude also helps us cope with crisis. Consciously cultivating an attitude of gratitude builds up a sort of psychological immune system that can cushion us when we fall."[59]

Building in this "cushion" means summoning that which we can be grateful for despite a most trying year.

What is there to be grateful for in 2020?

Reviewing this year might be draining, or outright exhausting. The year may have been devastating, especially if you've lost a loved one. Others may have lost their livelihoods, lost access to food or insurance, or aren't breathing as comfortably as they once did. If you've been directly affected, it might be especially trying to discover what to be grateful for this year.

The silver linings can multiply, if one tries to find, look for, and see them. Here are seven things to be grateful for from this challenging year, hopefully for all of us.

1. The connection with another human being. Indeed, in the midst of COVID, the connection with one another kicks in by default because we are all affected by the pandemic. As the poet Saadi states:

   Human beings are members of a whole
   In creation of one essence and soul
   If one member is afflicted with pain
   Other members uneasy will remain
   If you have no sympathy for human pain
   The name of human you cannot retain.[60]

   Saadi's words reflect a palpable bond that connects each of us with one another. In 2020, the year of COVID, we can be grateful for this special bond.
2. One breath in, one breath out. Again, with each breath in and each breath out, life continues. As the poet Saadi reflects on these two blessings reflecting life's continuation in man, he claims we cannot be grateful enough. To say thanks for each breath in and each breath out is impossible for man. In the year of COVID, many affected are not able to breathe as

easily. However, for those able to still continue living, we can be ever grateful for these two constant gifts.

3. Your body can take in food. For those whose lives continue, the ability to take in nutrients and water is something to be grateful for. The ability to take in food is a function of our bodies most of us take for granted. Yet, in the year of COVID (and also after), we can be grateful for this great gift.
4. You are able to get some sleep or rest. Without sleep, the body fails to perform its basic functions. The ability to sleep is something to be especially grateful for as our bodies continue to weather the signs of the pandemic.
5. You are able to grow as a person. This year, while many have lost jobs or businesses, and paychecks have been cut, it is especially hard to find ways to stay resilient. Yet, the biggest gift inside each human being is the ability to gain wisdom. Despite infection, physical limitations, or other ailments, humans are by their innate nature able to grow from experiences. This year, the ability to stay resilient and grow as human beings is something to hopefully be grateful for.
6. Gratitude for frontline workers. The dedication and perseverance of frontline workers is to be admired and appreciated by all both during 2020 and beyond. Grocery store workers, healthcare professionals, delivery personnel, first responders, caregivers, public health professionals, and more are most deserving of our respect and gratitude. Without them, daily living would be much more complicated and seemingly impossible. Thank you.

7. Gratitude for a vaccine. While many have received the COVID vaccine (and some haven't), we can still appreciate the discovery of one in 2020. Advancements in science enabling such a development are unprecedented. The achievements of COVID vaccines are worthy of our gratitude for the preservation of societies worldwide

COVID has brought challenge after challenge, seemingly ongoing. Still, we can be grateful for these seven things. What were you grateful for in 2020?

(*Psychology Today*, December 2020)

GRATITUDE BUILDS RESILIENCE IN THE HARDEST OF TIMES

"Resilience" is broadly defined by the Oxford Dictionary as "the ability of people to recover quickly from something unpleasant." Surely the experience of COVID has been unpleasant for most if not all. Is it possible to recover at all, let alone quickly? What does it mean to "recover" from the impact of COVID, even in the absence of disease?

For those who have lost loved ones, resilience means continuing on with their lives with patience and strength. Others who have not lost loved ones continue to live with difficult, subpar living conditions. Resilience means finding ways to adjust, move on, possibly succeed in terms of goals, and more. Gratitude can play a role here.

Here are three ways gratitude can help build resilience in the hardest of times.

1. GRATITUDE SUPPORTS ACTIVE COPING.

Active coping is when an individual finds a way to work with stressors and reaction to stressors in daily living. Gratitude supports active coping[61] by enabling people to approach a problem rather than avoiding one.[62] For example, if parenting during COVID has been particularly stressful, gratitude for having kids may encourage parents to play or interact with them and thereby support kids' well-being in new ways. Resilience here is gratitude-based by reconsidering what is clearly valued in one's life and subsequently finding new practices of strength to bring satisfaction and joy into pandemic living.

2. GRATITUDE CAN HELP THOSE WHO'VE EXPERIENCED TRAUMA AND VICE-VERSA.

Gratitude has been shown to lead to post-traumatic growth and well-being, and vice-versa—trauma has also been seen to induce gratefulness in people. A study looking at individuals losing a parent early in life revealed that gratitude helped lower depression. At the same time, 79 percent of those who lost a parent in childhood reported gaining an appreciation for life.[63]

For most, COVID has brought fatigue, if not trauma, for most, which can be aided via gratitude. On the flip side, COVID's impact may have helped us gain an appreciation for things small and big.

3. GRATITUDE BUILDS RESILIENCE FOR STUDENTS WHO FIND LEARNING CHALLENGING.

Gratitude has also been shown to help students build resilience toward learning. A study looking at this found that gratitude reminders via text helped students gain focus and put more effort into learning.[64] The virtual environment for kids and young adults is challenging enough to warrant gratitude as a helpful ingredient.

Gratitude's ability to shift perspective in the midst of stress, trauma, and more is significant. By building resilience in the hardest of times, gratitude facilitates strength, motivation, and active problem-solving.

COVID has brought very hard times, and gratitude is one of the tools that can help us see the way out and thrive.

What are some ways you can practice gratitude?

- Write a gratitude post on a social media platform, like the Gratitude Circle app (which is free!).
- Show your appreciation for a supportive friend.
- Share a story of appreciation for a past achievement in writing or in a conversation.

(*Psychology Today*, December 2020)

GRATITUDE PROTECTS AGAINST DEPRESSION

COVID may be impacting daily living, but gratitude can help fight back. Scientific research supports the finding that gratitude protects against depression. A couple of the common feelings among individuals facing depression include the following thoughts.

- "I am bothered by things that usually don't bother me."
- "I feel I could not shake off the blues even with the help from my family and friends."[65]

Multiple factors play a role in causing depression, including stress and lack of self-care. The research in the past several years has shown gratitude to be a protective factor. Below are three ways that gratitude helps protect against depression.

1. GRATITUDE BUFFERS AGAINST FEELINGS OF INADEQUACY.

In an Italian study, researchers found that gratitude positively strengthens how we view ourselves.[66] By reducing self-criticism and being more forgiving of ourselves, gratitude buffers against feelings of inadequacy. Researchers emphasize that gratitude "is connected to a less critical, less punishing, and more compassionate relationship with the self." In turn, when frustrations and challenges ensue, gratitude keeps individuals from being too hard on themselves.

Depression involves negative views of the self,[67] which can spiral into low self-esteem and even self-hate in severe forms. Gratitude's ability to protect against a negative self-view is not only helpful for those facing depression or depressive symptoms but almost anyone who may face a challenging day or set of circumstances. In short, gratitude can be psychologically protective for almost anyone.

In the above Italian study, gratitude was measured via a questionnaire with examples describing intensity, frequency, span, and density facets of gratitude such as the following.

- "I feel thankful for what I have received in life." (example of the intensity facet)
- "Long amounts of time can go by before I feel grateful to something or someone." (example of the frequency facet)
- "I sometimes feel grateful for the smallest things." (example of the span facet)
- "I am grateful to a wide variety of people." (example of the density facet)

2. GRATITUDE SUPPORTS PEACE OF MIND.

In a Chinese study, researchers concluded that gratitude may "counteract the symptoms of depression by enhancing a state of peace of mind and reducing ruminative thinking."[68] The study looked at a sample of roughly 500 Chinese university students. The results did not differ by gender; in other words, both males and females benefited equally from gratitude.

To add clarity, within Chinese culture, "peace of mind" has been defined as "a harmonious state of happiness."[69] Such research supports the positive role that gratitude can play by enhancing the naturally satisfactory balance of chemicals within the brain, developing peace and less stress.

3. GRATITUDE PROTECTS AGAINST DEPRESSION IN CHRONICALLY ILL PATIENTS ALSO.

In chronically ill populations facing arthritis or inflammatory bowel disease (IBD), gratitude still protects against depression. A study in *Health Psychology* found that gratitude was associated with lower levels of depression in individuals facing either IBD or arthritis.[70] Study participants completed a gratitude questionnaire that reflected how much they noticed and were appreciative of the positive in life. Such findings support the notion that despite physical ailments, gratitude still uniquely strengthens the mind.

Gratitude's benefits include strengthening relationships, minimizing stress, strengthening empathy, serving as a gateway to more positive emotions, and protecting against depression. The benefits start but do not necessarily end here. A routine gratitude practice can impart such benefits even if gratitude does not come naturally. Attempting to feel gratitude through a gratitude habit may take effort, particularly in the wake of a pandemic, but the rewards are ever worth the effort.

(*Psychology Today*, December 2020)

GRATITUDE HELPS STRENGTHEN HOW WE MAKE OTHERS FEEL

In the age of the Internet and mobile apps, the chance to make others feel valued in our relationships may not come often enough. As psychologist and philosopher William James once said, "The deepest craving of human nature is the need to be appreciated." Gratitude for loved ones, spouses, friends, and other close relationships is often recognized by how their words and actions make us feel. Recognizing the importance of how we feel in relationships can then be a motivator to make others in relationships feel valued, appreciated, good, encouraged, and believed in. Beyond simply out of an intention to flatter, making others feel all these good ways has the ability to change people's perspective, uplift them, change them for the better, and so many other possible good outcomes.

Below are three ways how you can make others feel in order to strengthen your relationships.

1. VALUED AND APPRECIATED

Gratefulness develops in relationships where we feel genuinely valued. This begins with our relationship with ourselves. Self-value means placing interest in our good qualities; maintaining gratefulness for our abilities and strengths; and engaging in positive self-talk.

Beyond ourselves, our immediate circles of family, friends, coworkers, colleagues, and more have potential to make us feel valued. Such relationships grow over time and require effort. With our focus on helping the other people in our relationships feel valued, we can shift our attention to our words and actions in these relationships. Why not acknowledge others' milestones, achievements, and character from a genuine place? This can add depth and breadth to the relationship. It can make others feel good and valued. By appreciating the feeling of being valued by others, we can reciprocate the words, actions, and behavior in return. Not simply because it's a good thing to do (which can be true, too), but because making others feel valued and appreciated is a principle you value.

2. GOOD

The ability to make another feel that they are "good"—that they have an innately good nature—is priceless. For parents, this is one of the best ways to make your kids genuinely feel, which can have positive effects by leaps and bounds. If a child feels "good," they can feel comfortable in themselves and remain true to who they are, which can be the best parenting lesson of all.

Whether you think another deserves to be made to feel "good" could come into question. If so, just remember that pain and love are felt by all, though personalities vary distinctly and life circumstances come in different shapes and sizes for all. Just as well, individuals react differently to various opportunities and challenges. Making a person feel good might give them the chance to shine through.

3. ENCOURAGED AND BELIEVED IN

Teachers can motivate their students to go for their dreams. What if this motivation was given out freely and, at the same time, genuinely? People would line up to be motivated, especially when no one in their familiar orbit is dishing out the support. For those you care about, encouraging words about their character, strengths, and more are priceless. Keep in mind these should come from a genuine place. While affirming someone's character today is important, even more important is encouraging them as they grow, heal, and change for the better. Teaching this resilience reflects an understanding of the storms and fragility of life. Look at it this way: Reminding someone that they can always grow and change for the better is like giving them a winning lottery ticket—that person can do anything with hard work, practice, and patience.

Want to get started on developing the great skill of making others feel wonderful? Try these three suggestions.

1. Forgive and focus on making others feel all these great ways (see above). Beginning the new year with optimism for your relationships might be just what you need.
2. Plant the seeds of supportive words and actions within all your circles, especially those that matter most to you.
3. Don't worry if the feeling is not reciprocated at first. Remember, people have different ways of reacting to genuine support and kindness. The fact that you tried instills the habit and helps develop a sense of altruism as a guiding principle for you.

(*Psychology Today*, January 2021)

GRATITUDE AND TECHNOLOGY: A POWERFUL ANTIDOTE

Technology in our modern era enables self-empowerment as an everyday exercise. What does that mean? Mobile apps have promoted regular use of mindfulness, meditation, physical exercise, and gratitude, to name a few such practices.

Gratitude, specifically, has been studied for nearly two decades (since the early '00s). Gratitude has shown via research to:

- reduce stress[71]
- improve sleep
- lower risk for anxiety[72]
- lower risk for depression[73]
- strengthen relationships[74]
- boost immunity
- improve self-esteem
- increase social and emotional learning[75]

While not all studies show significant improvements in well-being with gratitude, dozens of studies point towards gratitude being a gateway to better mental, physical, social, and emotional health. Gratitude has been shown to promote life satisfaction, and the association between the two even includes a neural basis.[76] Gratitude increases dopamine and serotonin levels[77] in the brain, which are key neurotransmitters that give us feelings of contentment.[78]

What role does technology play in the use of gratitude?

Social media apps today are being used at an exorbitant scale, with 45 percent of teens ages thirteen to seventeen years being online "constantly."[79] The role that mobile phones and apps play in our lives, however, does not need to be all-consuming or negative. Positive social media apps can become increasingly captivating and inspiring, especially if we intend them to be that way.

By molding gratitude-centered platforms to look and function similar to Facebook and Instagram, technology plus gratitude can become a powerful antidote to stress and negativity that often tip exceedingly high.

The self-empowerment modality, in the form of a mobile app, has been taken advantage of by many apps, such as Headspace, Calm, and others. These successful apps show the dire need for relaxation, focus, self-regulation, and other aspects of emotional intelligence. What's next? A booming, inspirational, and positively engaging gratitude app. The potential? To reach and bridge communication among a global population, inspire each of us to "pay it forward," and allow each individual to soak up their share of life satisfaction. Gratitude has the potential to do that, especially if we see and seize the opportunity. My app, the Gratitude Circle app, is the platform which carries the potential to promise self-empowerment globally.

In a 2020 study[80] in *The Journal of Positive Psychology*, gratitude's role in promoting academic performance and well-being was highlighted among high school students. Students used a gratitude social media (web) app called GiveThx at least twice a day for six weeks.

Millennials have an exceedingly high interest in social entrepreneurship, and in connecting globally; this demand comes at a time when technology can do that on a wide scale. The researched benefits of gratitude, when blended into captivating technology, can become beneficial to billions. The impact: Health and well-being can expand at a tremendous scale with the right app, simultaneously fostering and enriching cross-cultural communication and promoting a better world.[81]

With the right combination of gratitude and technology, the Gratitude Circle app can be a powerful antidote to the world's trauma, suffering, loneliness, and negativity. At the end of the day, we can be proud to have technology infused with gratitude and positivity as a self-serving tool, self-empowering and brightening the world for each of us, one everyday gratitude exercise and inspiration at a time.

(*Psychology Today*, February 2021)

4 WAYS TO WIRE YOUR BRAIN FOR GRATITUDE

There are many different ways to express gratitude—be it a quick "thanks," a heartfelt card, or maybe a favor in return. No matter how you express it, being mindful of the moments when you feel grateful can rewire your brain for the better. Research has found that simply feeling grateful, even if you don't necessarily share those feelings with anyone, can boost your mental health in the long run and have lasting effects on the brain.[82] Furthermore, expressing and accepting gratitude[83] from others can strengthen your relationship and your overall sense of well-being.

Here are four ways to train your brain to practice more gratitude.

1. TAKE TIME TO NOTICE WHAT'S AROUND YOU.

Practicing mindfulness helps you tune in to the present moment. It is possible that if you are a grateful person, you are more mindful of others' gestures. The more often you tune into your awareness, the greater the chances you will notice all the good that's around you to feel gratitude for, which can then bring satisfaction and happiness. Our ability to pick up on the beauty of nature, kindness from one another, and the chance to make a living via a job all require our ability to be cognizant of ourselves and our surroundings. Being mindful of help in the kitchen, or the color of the sky, allows us to generate gratitude by simply *noticing* them.

2. PRACTICE GRATITUDE FOR THE LITTLE THINGS.

We often remember to be grateful for big events, like graduating from university or getting married, but it can be more difficult to feel grateful for the small things we do every day. Reminding yourself that eating a meal is special in itself, for example, can be very powerful. Your immediate awareness of the food in front of you, combining flavors while removing hunger, is a great way to enjoy gratitude as often as you eat! Another example is feeling grateful in the morning for being able to comfortably sleep at night. We gain comfort, satisfaction, and peace by practicing mindfulness and gratitude in this repeated fashion.

3. SHARE YOUR GRATITUDE FOR YOUR LOVED ONES.

Most of us are a little bit guilty of taking our loved ones for granted. The next time you notice a kind act by a loved one, why not show gratitude by simply saying "thank you" or giving them a hug? We ought to show appreciation and not let kind acts go unnoticed. Training yourself to show your gratefulness for loved ones can strengthen your relationships.

4. SPREAD GRATITUDE VIA YOUR SOCIAL MEDIA PLATFORMS.

Social media can feel so negative at times, but using it to share your gratitude can help create a more positive online atmosphere. For example, share an uplifting moment from a recent event, or a lesson you learned from a book you read, or a photo of a place nearby that you're grateful for. Spreading good, and in a unique and uplifting way, is one way we can each do our part in this digital age to remind one another that we have a lot to be grateful for. Let us each inspire each other in this way.

Training our minds to practice gratitude more often is possible if we are mindful of ourselves, each other, and our environment. Let us widen our circle of appreciation and reap the benefits of gratitude.

(*Mindful.org*, November 2019)

HOW TO TURN GRATITUDE INTO A LIFESTYLE

Being grateful has numerous researched benefits, including health, happiness, fulfillment, and more. What can prompt us to turn gratitude into a lifestyle, if it is so rewarding? Here are five ways you can infuse gratitude into your everyday routine.

1. CONSIDER GRATITUDE WHEN YOU FEEL A NEGATIVE EMOTION.

A setback or challenge can be turned around more quickly if we are grateful for it. Consider gratitude the next time you feel a negative emotion. Tell yourself, "It's okay I feel this way; maybe there's a reason for it, and I am grateful for that." You may be feeling down, irritated, angry, or frustrated. Perhaps being grateful for the emotion will let you turn your mood around. By considering gratitude in the moment, you have become stronger and all the wiser.

2. PRACTICE GRATITUDE WHEN YOU EMBRACE SUCCESS.

Success comes for all of us in different forms. Indeed, we can be grateful when it does come our way. Humbly embracing success with open gratitude can make the feeling all that richer. For example, receiving a job offer can be a great time to recall gratitude. Scores of interviews later, you are settled on a new pursuit. Doesn't the reward feel great? Even greater with gratitude? Recall the journey you have taken and abundance, wisdom, and joy will fill your heart.

3. MINDFULLY CHOOSE GRATEFULNESS TO HELP YOU MAKE A BIGGER DECISION.

If you are making a tough decision, consider which path will be rewarded with more gratefulness. If you are choosing between jobs perhaps, or choosing a life partner, considering what will fill you with gratitude more can help you in carefully deciding among options. Be grateful, be thoughtful, be wise, and be accepting. Opportunity will find you, to fill your pocket and heart, if you steer with gratitude in mind.

4. REMEMBER GRATITUDE WHEN YOU RECEIVE A COMPLIMENT.

A list of what you are grateful for is great. You can be more mindful of the smaller and bigger joys that fill your day, including compliments. We may receive compliments on clothes, work performance, and more without even appreciating them at times. When we practice a grateful lifestyle, however, our minds tune into everything positive (reversing also the negative) and compliments feel that much more rewarding. Try a regular gratitude practice and you'll be pleasantly surprised by how fulfilling compliments (and relationships with those who give them) can actually feel!

5. REMIND LOVED ONES OF THE REWARDS GRATITUDE CAN BRING TO HELP THEM OUT.

Reminding others to feel grateful for all they have in subtle ways often can be an uplifting force. Being uplifting and looking to the positive can help others see things that way too. Encouraging others to empower with gratitude will undoubtedly bring more happiness into more lives (including yours).

Turning gratitude into a lifestyle can be difficult, but with regular practice, it is doable. Once it is doable, it can become a powerful way of living. The awe, joy, and wonder that the practice of gratitude can bring is invaluable. Try your hand at gratitude and see how awesome it feels.

(*GratCircle.com*, August 2020)

PART II

SELF-ESTEEM AND SELF-CONFIDENCE

5 WAYS TO BUILD AND MAINTAIN SELF-ESTEEM

Do you want to feel confident more often? Do you wish you had more self-esteem? If your answer is "yes," then perhaps you could use a slight boost in how you feel about yourself. Below are five ways to help you build and maintain self-esteem.

1. KEEP WORKING HARD TOWARD YOUR GOALS.

When you might feel uncertain about which direction you're taking with respect to work, your relationships, or your personal growth, remember to keep working hard toward your goals. Persistence day-in and day-out will ultimately keep your achievements flowing, which can be a great boost to self-esteem.

2. LET YOURSELF FEEL.

What does this mean? If you're facing a challenge, don't hesitate to let yourself feel the range of emotions that might flow through you. Remember, identifying and even wrestling with even negative emotions can drive your personal growth. Don't dwell on the difficult emotions, however. Focus on the upside of things, but remember to let yourself feel.

3. ATTACH YOUR GOALS TO SOMETHING GREATER THAN YOURSELF.

When we feel down, the focus might be too much on ourselves. Attaching goals to a mission greater than you (e.g., volunteering) will help you focus on others and can be a reminder to be kind, respectful, and mindful of what others are going through, too. This can be easier said than done, however.

Consider this. A simple gesture such as asking how a person's day or week went can show that you care. By fostering empathy and kindness for others this way, you can broaden your perspective on your own challenges and feel grateful for your achievements, opportunities, and relationships.

4. PRACTICE SELF-CARE.

When you are at a crossroads for how you can help yourself, remember to take care of your body and mind. Practicing self-care might mean a trip to the gym, following a beloved recipe, or getting a good night's sleep. Whatever you need, try to generate good habits with respect to self-care to boost your self-esteem regularly.

5. REMEMBER, THE FUTURE IS YOURS FOR THE TAKING.

When you dwell on difficulties, past or present, you can lose sight of what the future can bring. Perhaps the future will bring a new friend or addition to your family. Whatever it is, the plentiful positive and bright possibilities are yours for the taking and can help you eliminate doubts or troubles that might limit your self-esteem. Focusing on the bright possibilities of the future can offer tremendous hope, regardless of what the past holds.

In total, these five ways can help you boost and maintain your self-esteem whenever you might need a little refocusing. Keep your head held high, and keep working hard!

(*The Huffington Post*, November 2017)

3 TIPS TO KEEP SELF-DOUBT AT BAY AND BE A "CHARACTER BUTTERFLY"

Dr. Maya Angelou, American poet and civil rights activist, once said, "If you're always trying to be normal, you will never know how amazing you can be." So, in light of Dr. Angelou's words, it might be worth asking yourself: Do you care too much what others think about you? Are you fearful of criticism? Do you want to feel free of worry?

First of all, you're in the company of many. We have been wired to care about what people think of us in order to preserve the quality of our relationships and, as a result, our satisfaction and chances for survival.[84] However, overdoing it can be preoccupying and unnecessary.

Try these tips to keep self-doubt at bay and be what I call a "character butterfly." What is a "character butterfly"? Essentially, rather than the "social butterfly" we may have heard of, a "character butterfly," I would say, is one who has the courage to be their most authentic self, driven with purpose to do good and help others. Try these three tips to start with.

1. USE SELF-CRITICISM OR CRITICISM FROM OTHERS TO DRIVE YOU AHEAD.

In the last few days before her husband left office, then-First Lady Michelle Obama sat down with Oprah Winfrey for an interview and gave advice to young girls everywhere about how to cope with negativity and unfair criticism: Use it to fuel you forward.[85] Based on her time in the limelight, the previous FLOTUS offered the wisdom that helped her to build campaigns around fitness, diet, and more. While most of us may not receive the level of attention that the First Lady did, we can still certainly use her advice while charting our own paths.

If you want to stop being bothered by what others are thinking of you, or if you are overly self-critical, try to collect those thoughts, and use them to fuel you, rather than making you preoccupied. Your success, and your efforts, will give you the confidence you need to showcase your most amazing traits.

2. PURSUE ACHIEVEMENTS THAT WILL MAKE YOU TRULY HAPPY—NOT JUST SO OTHERS WILL PRAISE YOU.

Professor Raj Raghunathan at the University of Texas at Austin, who teaches a course on happiness, found that consistently ranked at the top of people's list of what they want to learn from his course is this: "I would like to learn how to stop being bothered by what others are thinking of me."[86]

So, considering the consequences of this common feeling, are people pursuing goals in life just to get praise and respect from others? Yes, in part. Should you still work towards achievements that will truly make you happier? Definitely, yes. While competition in life can be healthy, remember that pursuing things that will truly make you happier will be more fulfilling and could potentially touch people's lives in helpful ways. Rather than chasing materialistic goods or achievements solely to get praise from others, consider what will genuinely drive your happiness and satisfaction.

3. REMEMBER THAT SELF-DOUBT CAN FUEL DEEPER HAPPINESS WITH APPROPRIATE REFLECTION.

This point may be harder to acknowledge. With enough reflection on, but without overanalyzing difficult emotions, you can feel more lasting happiness. How? Science writer Matthew Hutson writes in *Psychology Today*, "We have the wrong idea about emotions. They're very rational; they're means to help us achieve goals important to us, tools carved by eons of human experience that work beyond conscious awareness to direct us where we need to go. They identify trouble or opportunity and suggest methods of repair or gain."[87]

So, while unpleasant, self-doubt and other negative emotions can result in measurable progress (i.e., "repair" or "gain"). From time to time, we may need a little self-doubt to drive us forward to even greater success. The trick is to recognize the helpfulness *of the process*. Perhaps by writing down or talking about our "bumps in the road," we can look back and realize we are making progress.

All in all, in this short piece, there are three tips to keep self-doubt at bay: 1) Use criticism to move you forward, 2) Pursue things that will truly make you happy, and 3) Remember that long-lasting happiness requires some self-doubt or other “bumpy” emotions. Hopefully, these tips can help you keep self-doubt at bay and be your own “character butterfly”!

(*The Huffington Post*, July 2017)

HOW TO LET GO OF YOUR INSECURITIES

Has doubt, worry, anxiety, or frustration ever got you in a slump? If so, perhaps you might consider what to do to become free from, or better manage, your insecurities. Try these six suggestions.

1. DO WHAT YOU CAN TO PREPARE YOURSELF FOR A LIFE GUIDED BY PURPOSE.

When we feel caught up in our insecurities, it may be because the direction we're taking in life is not as clear, or we lack the preparation to fully live out that purpose. Being courageous enough to determine your purpose is the first step. Preparing to live out that purpose is the next.

2. REMEMBER TO NURTURE YOUR PHYSICAL AND MENTAL WELL-BEING.

However successful we may feel, if our bodies—either physically or mentally—suffer, then we are not succeeding in the most optimal way. Eating a variety of healthy foods, building a strong social network, sleeping enough, and exercising are good ways to nurture yourself. Relieving tension through an honest conversation with a friend or loved one could be another. With these suggestions and more, you can start to take care of yourself in order to truly enjoy success and happiness.

3. COLLECT AND CHANNEL THE POSITIVE INTO YOUR WORDS AND ACTIONS.

If there's a regular source leading to any of your insecurity, you need to pause and find a way to let go of it. For example, you may have a rude coworker who you ought to ignore, if possible. Remember to collect all the positive influences around you, words of encouragement, and your wisdom, and channel them into words of kindness and good actions.

4. BE YOUR NATURAL SELF AND AS CAREFREE AS YOUR SURROUNDINGS ALLOW YOU.

The best remedy to many of our insecurities is being natural—in other words, doing less overthinking or worrying. When we let go, we can leave a sparkly trail of glitter behind. Remind yourself that the more you exercise your carefree side, the more likely insecurities can fade away and you appreciate your authentic self more.

5. FIGURE OUT YOUR STRENGTHS, AND KEEP USING THEM.

Often our insecurities get the best of us when we're not practicing our strengths. If we regularly hone in on our strengths and use them often, there's less room for worry, doubt, anxiety, or frustration. Try to figure out your biggest strength, repeatedly use it, and see how much happiness and joy you get in return!

6. FORGET COMPARING YOURSELF TO OTHERS.

The worse (albeit difficult to avoid) sabotage to our uniqueness is the comparison to others. Make it a point to limit or eliminate comparisons that won't leave you or others feeling any better.

In all, these six suggestions can help put you on a path to feeling less insecure. Just like most good things, practice helps, so take time, and when you feel more secure, and satisfied, you'll know it.

(*GratCircle.com*, March 2018)

5 WAYS TO LET YOURSELF SHINE BRIGHTER

Have you ever considered you are too hard on yourself? That you were keeping your character or personality from shining brighter? Oftentimes, we may critique ourselves too harshly, when we, in fact, have unbridled potential. Remember the importance of self-love, self-value, and self-confidence with these five ways to let yourself shine brighter.

1. REMEMBER POSITIVE MOMENTS, AND BUILD YOUR SELF-CONFIDENCE FOR FUTURE ENDEAVORS ON THESE MEMORIES.

Olympic figure skater Michelle Kwan once described the way she gained her confidence and composure before each and every performance: She said she went over her past successful performances in her mind, training herself to collect confidence and enthusiasm.

While it may be hard at times, try to focus on positive events in your past. When you might be feeling overly self-critical, remind yourself of these. Consider how great it would be to keep building upward and outward, rather than being unforgiving and unfair to yourself and losing sight of what you can achieve. If you feel like there aren't enough positive moments, you might create them by daydreaming. Visualize where you want to be, and work on goals to help you get there.

2. LET YOURSELF SHINE BASED ON YOUR CHARACTER OR PERSONALITY, AND TRY NOT TO RELY ON MATERIALISTIC GOODS.

While a good facial, designer outfit, or nice car could help you look and feel great, one of the best ways to lock in star power is to build it from within. Material goods such as clothing, footwear, and makeup may be a great way to showcase your inner light, but be wary that relationships cannot be necessarily or solely based on appearances. The best-quality relationships will likely come from letting others get a glimpse of your valuable character and personality. As Oprah Winfrey famously quoted Dr. Maya Angelou in a recent commencement address, "Your legacy is every life you've touched."[88]

3. KEEP ON NURTURING THE RELATIONSHIPS THAT YOU FIND AS THE MOST SUPPORTING, ENCOURAGING, AND POSITIVE.

Quality relationships are the ones you can't get enough of, because you know the other person genuinely cares for you. Indeed, the best relationships are like beautiful flowers: You'll feel compelled to nourish them so you can feel the beauty and light and they bring with them.

By nurturing such relationships, your light will grow brighter also. The positivity and support you gain will help you feel understood, respected, appreciated and ready to give back to others in wider social circles. Your light, your impact will be felt far outside your inner ties once you begin to make others feel encouraged and supported.

4. PRACTICE GOOD HABITS SUCH AS SELF-CARE, ONGOING LEARNING, AND GOOD MANNERS, INCLUDING GIVING THANKS.

For any person who wants to shine brighter (i.e., through their personas and character), these simple, everyday habits are a must. If you have trouble with these, try to pick up one habit at a time.

Self-care will help you feel and look great. Continued learning can keep your brain young and active, while also seeding wisdom. In fact, there is reduced cognitive decline among those who continue learning into old age.[89] And good manners, including giving thanks, give you a lot to feel good about, since these reflect caring, politeness, and respect. In fact, according to successful entrepreneur Mark Ford, the key to getting what you want in life without offending people is good manners.[90]

5. GROW YOUR CAPACITY TO BE MINDFUL.

What is mindfulness? According to one definition, it is the "quality or state of being conscious or aware of something."

Why is it important? Growing our capacity to be mindful might include mindfulness meditation. According to Harvard Medical School neuroscientist Sara Lazar, mindfulness meditation fosters a better understanding of ourselves and others, greater resilience under stress, and emotional strength. Such traits can help us embrace life, create more happiness, and be a brighter light to those around us!

Try these five ways to let yourself shine brighter to those around you—if not all of them at once, try adopting one at a time. Surely, with practice, diligence, and time, you will touch more lives.

(*The Huffington Post*, June 2017)

12 WAYS TO BELIEVE YOU CAN DO WHAT YOU SET YOUR MIND TO

Do you feel tired, or even drained at times? How often do you feel like you can do whatever it is you set your mind to?

Here are twelve ways to remind yourself, and actually believe, that you can do what it is you set your mind to—whether that is taking better care of yourself, getting that promotion, or whatever you are in pursuit of.

1. BELIEVING YOU CAN TAKES YOU HALFWAY THERE.

Never underestimate the power of self-belief. From seasoned athletes to CEOs of billion-dollar companies, each person's journey most often starts, and is guided, through pure self-belief. When you get up in the morning, if you feel motivated for your day, that itself is a sign of self-belief. If this is an area you're struggling with, consider your personal and professional paths. Perhaps these need some tweaking or redirecting. If you're already motivated with what you do every day, this can be quite helpful. Getting over the bottlenecks or plateaus of your days, weeks, or months can be somewhat less challenging. Believing you can doesn't mean you won't fail. It just gives more fuel for the ultimate marathon of life. Some days will be hard for all of us, no matter your degree of self-belief.

2. HOPE CAN CARRY YOU INTO UNHEARD-OF SUCCESS.

Build hope, and see how it can carry you into unheard-of success. Haven't you heard the phrase, "If you can dream it, you can reach it?" If not, now you have.

Oprah Winfrey said, "Create the highest, grandest vision possible for your life, because you become what you believe." Keeping hope through any difficulty, however hard, will help get you through it. Simply: Hope.

3. FOCUS, WHILE ENJOYING WHAT YOU DO.

Sometimes, we may keep working hard without focus. This drains us and keeps us from enjoying what we do. Focus in a way that will let you enjoy what you're presently doing. Consider how good working out will make you feel, during and after. Consider how you'll nourish your body with a healthy meal. Instead of seeing difficulty, let your perspective be guided by how you'll benefit from each next activity.

4. TAKE IT EASY, THE WAY YOU KNOW HOW.

Haven't you heard, "Just take it easy," like a million times? What does that even mean? If each of us took it easy, in the sense of "not doing anything," we'd all be lazy and unproductive. I say, take it easy the way you know how. If you're running around doing errands all day, you might treat yourself to a nice dinner. Whatever way, practice self-care and self-love often in healthy and reinvigorating ways, and you'll be the master of taking it easy.

5. RAISE YOUR SELF-ESTEEM BY PURSUING EXCELLENCE, NOT PERFECTION.

If we each could do everything we wanted, without failure or rejection, there would be less value in the purpose of excellence. Part of the journey towards excellence, or what could be seen as thoroughness at times, is to be prepared to rebuild or raise our self-esteem when we fall down. For example, let's say you failed a course in a past semester. The next semester, by pursuing growth or excellence in your new courses, you will help raise your self-esteem. Since all of us fall at one point or another, make small or big mistakes, having the mindset that you can make a comeback for things big and small, is critical to success in life. Pursue this type of "raising-your-game" excellence, not perfection.

6. KEEP TRYING, WITH PRECISION AND POLITE CONSIDERATION THAT OTHERS HAVE A LOT GOING ON.

When reaching out to others to get, say, an internship or job, keep trying, but with polite consideration that others have a lot going on. Also, be precise in explaining what you want. Ask clearly and politely. You'll eventually steer yourself towards plentiful success!

7. DON'T SHY AWAY FROM A BOLD, BUT PRAGMATIC MOVE.

What, you say? How do I know when to be bold, but pragmatic? It's usually when you feel in your gut that it's the right thing to do! For example, you might ask for a raise, politely and after a reasonable amount of time. This kind of assertiveness is what steers some of us towards success that others don't see possible or attainable.

8. CELEBRATE YOUR JOURNEY WHEN THE TIME CALLS FOR IT!

Sometimes, kicking back and, say, dancing to your favorite song can be the perfect celebration for mini and major achievements. You'll have added belief that you are on the right path by adding fun and joy!

9. TAKE SOME TIME OUT WHEN YOU NEED TO.

If you need a break from working too hard, take it. Breaks may help you get newfound perspective, motivation, and energy. You will be thankful you did!

10. REVISIT ACTIVITIES THAT MAKE YOU FEEL GOOD.

When working toward a goal—any goal—make some time to do activities that make you feel good. For example, you might watch your favorite television show or cook your favorite recipe. This type of reengagement of your mind in rewarding activities will help you recharge and refocus.

11. TREAT OTHERS KINDLY AND RESPECTFULLY DURING THE PURSUIT.

Without thinking too hard about it, think about how you'd want others to treat you. Many of us prefer to be treat kindly and respectfully, which you can aim to reciprocate in your relationships. Your meaningful treatment will usually reinforce your personal and professional objectives, helping you achieve what you want.

12. LET YOURSELF ENJOY THE PURSUIT.

If, overall, you're not enjoying the pursuit of a long-term or short-term goal, perhaps it's not meant for you. A new pursuit can be challenging, so if difficult at first, you can tell if you're growth is satisfying enough to continue. If you are enjoying the pursuit on the whole, then simply hold onto those rewarding moments and enjoy!

These are twelve ways to keep you believing you can do what you set your mind to. I hope you find out for yourself how good they feel!

(*GratCircle.com,* April 2019)

5 TIPS TO EXUDE CONFIDENCE IN YOUR CHARACTER

Do you struggle with being confident? Are you interested in feeling and projecting more confidence? Try these five tips.

1. LEARN TO SAY "NO" WHEN YOU MEAN IT.

If you feel like you're asked to do a certain chore or task that feels like it's too much for you, remember you can say "no" when you mean it. Knowing your own limits does not make you less of a people-pleaser. It means you understand your capabilities and emotional threshold, so that you don't ruin your mood, and you can stay on top of the chores, errands, and tasks that you can handle and do very well. Gently setting boundaries can show you are emotionally self-aware and uniquely confident. Also, if you accept too much, you can let others down by not being able to deliver what was asked for, either totally or partially.

2. SEIZE OPPORTUNITIES THAT WILL LET YOU SHINE.

Wouldn't the world be more beautiful if we each excelled at what we were each truly good at? A certain task may be easy for you, but for someone else it could be very difficult. For example, if you are a great makeup artist, try to put on the right "look" for specific occasions to make you feel pretty. Using the best moisturizer may be your secret. Perhaps sparkling with lip gloss is your trademark touch. Whatever the case, you can project confidence when you seize an opportunity to show off your skill of applying makeup. Try figuring out two or three things you are particularly good at, and consistently apply your talents to allow yourself to look and feel confident.

3. CHART YOUR OWN PATH TO SUCCESS.

Charting your own path to success means you are not deceitful, you do not exploit others for personal gain, and you are respectful of others. This requires hard work and routine patience, but is ultimately more rewarding to your self-confidence and can strengthen grit and character.

4. TRY TO BE YOUR OWN SELF WHEN YOU FACE THE WORLD.

Yes, it shows grace and poise not to showcase every emotion to everyone we meet. However, being our own self in the right time and place can also be valuable to help us identify, validate, and express emotions that represent who we are. Consider carrying a balance between reserving deeper emotions and revealing your unique personality to help exude self-confidence.

5. LOVE YOURSELF FOR WHO YOU ARE WHILE RATIONALIZING SHORTCOMINGS AND DIFFICULT EMOTIONS.

Love your most positive traits, always. They are your gifts to the world. Rationalizing the parts you don't love about yourself can also help you *feel* more confidence. For example, if you feel self-doubt, perhaps you can attribute it to difficulty in your life such as a testing relationship. Challenges will come and go, so rationalizing temporary sources of upset, fatigue, stress, or heartache will keep you feeling balanced and positive—and *that* will feed into your growing self-confidence.

If you want to exude confidence, keep these tips in mind. They could be the beginning of your list or added to other tips you might have. Circumstances in life can shift your self-confidence towards highs or lows, which is normal, but what's important is to recognize these changes, persevere, go forward, and rebuild that confidence.

(*The Huffington Post*, October 2016)

JENNIFER LOPEZ, FIRST LADY MICHELLE OBAMA, AND MYSELF ON "FEELING COMFORTABLE IN YOUR OWN SKIN"

I won't forget an episode of the last season of *American Idol* when one of judge Jennifer Lopez's comments resonated with me. Reacting to a stellar performance, she said something to the effect of, "It's all about feeling comfortable in your own skin." She praised the contestant and passed on a lesson to me that night as well.

Isn't it all about feeling comfortable in our own skin? Certainly, as social beings we could feel the desire to be a part multiple social networks, whether they are through dinner parties, work meetings, brunches, picnics, book clubs, or any context, really. The message to feel assured about ourselves, our personalities, and our impact on others is a truly important one, and one that we might take time to reflect on so we can cultivate lasting comfort. How we feel about ourselves can amplify or limit our enjoyment in life and, more significantly, is a feeling that can contribute to great self-esteem if we value ourselves properly. Our impact on others can be shaped with a helpful dose of self-value and self-esteem, strengthening our ability to contribute meaningfully and effectively in society.

When I hear good advice, I like to share it to help others, and Ms. Lopez's words are a good example. I don't know if she came up with the advice herself, but at the time she spoke them, it did catch my attention.

A related strong piece of wisdom is the advice that First Lady Michelle Obama gave at the United State of Women Summit while being interviewed by Oprah Winfrey.[91] She talked about self-value and how the FLOTUS could not have done her job as First Lady as comfortably if she did she not have the self-value she's had for decades. While self-esteem is a concept we may feel we don't have control over at times, self-value is not like that. Self-value is based on our own set of values and whether we can strive to uphold them. Self-esteem, however, is transient and oftentimes dependent on mood and environment. We can influence our thoughts and perspective to shape a healthier self-value, which in turn can boost self-esteem. (You'll find more ways to boost self-esteem in *5 Ways to Build and Maintain Self-Esteem.*)

It is so important, especially in today's society, that we treat ourselves better than ever, because most others do not simply have the time to do so. We ought to care for and believe in our best traits in order to nourish our self-value. We ought to understand and accept that being human means we will have difficulties presented as well.

Loving yourself is as important as every other way we care for ourselves, like eating and sleeping. Being narcissistic is different, as achieving balance in self-value is important, just like finding balance in everything else in life is important. If you need to reflect on why you should love yourself, take some time and do the soul-searching. Keep at those things that make you feel the most self-confident; those habits and hobbies will likely reveal your biggest strengths and reasons to feel good about yourself.

Remember, we may be small in the bigger scheme of society and the world's affairs, but within each one of us lies a universe of our own to behold.

Here are two steps to follow if you want to develop greater *self-value* and feel comfortable in your own skin.

1. SHARE STRENGTHS WHICH REFLECT YOUR PERSONAL VALUES AS MUCH AS POSSIBLE.

When you are an active member of your social networks, it can create a positive feeling, especially if you're able to show off your strengths. You might be super thoughtful, kind, loving, bold and fierce, skilled at business, something else, or all the above. Going to events (while this could be tough in COVID times) and sharing views with others will let others get a feel for your character and mindset. By spreading your sphere of influence in good and positive ways, your self-value can increase.

2. BE ON THE LOOKOUT FOR GREAT ADVICE AND CONTINUOUS WAYS TO IMPROVE YOURSELF.

The journey to shaping our attitude and mindset will constantly shift based on life factors. Having the ability to adapt and be grateful in every circumstance will no doubt be a huge asset if you can. Love yourself, live gratefully, and dream big. Hopefully, with the ability to value your traits and personality, you can regularly "feel comfortable in your own skin," and continue to shine.

(*The Huffington Post*, September 2016)

LIFE FOUNDATIONS 101: APPRECIATING PERSONAL IDENTITY AND INTERNAL COPING MECHANISMS

How strong is your personal identity, or your appreciation of your inner qualities? Do you have internal coping mechanisms that keep you going? These are two critical questions we ought to be able to answer with confidence and strength. As life changes or throws us a curveball, our appreciation of our inner qualities and use of personal coping mechanisms can help navigate us through difficulty and uncertainty. That's why they are so important. Let's pick apart the first question in order to gain a deeper awareness of ourselves.

APPRECIATING PERSONAL IDENTITY

How strong is your personal identity or your appreciation of your inner qualities? Well, ask yourself this: Outside of your job, your income, your spouse or fiancé, your kids—would you still be able to appreciate yourself for who you really are? Do you fully embrace the fact that you are kind, loving, honest, helpful, and funny, or other traits?

If you find your overall appreciation wavering day-in and day-out—not your temporary mood—you might need to *reflect* on values that you truly care about and hold onto these. To name a few values, there is humility, honesty, and dependability. Strong values often form the basis of your greatest inner qualities. Now you name the values you hold dear to you.

Alternatively, you might need to be *reminded* of your greatest inner qualities. Listen to friends, family, or acquaintances who might describe the impact you have on others. If you think they may be biased, think again. They are the ones who know your worth. If you have a difficult living situation and find others' opinions way off, then you can ask a friend, neighbor or other relative for their thoughts.

For parents, getting kids to *engage in activities* that help channel and build positive inner qualities is a great way to build confidence early on. For example, if you want your kids to gain and appreciate self-discipline as an inner quality, you can encourage them to start exercising, or possibly play a sport. Joining a sport or activity with a friend from school can even help them learn how to build social networks outside of school. Being able to socialize effectively is a skill that can help develop better quality relationships for life. Ultimately, participating in rewarding activities will help kids to develop self-esteem, and to appreciate and likely engage their inner qualities for the rest of their lives.

As adults, if we affix a job, a relationship, or an income to our personal identity, we fall short of truly valuing ourselves. The greater part of society tells us to value *monetary* goods, such as a house or car; or *materialistic* goods, such as a fancy dress; or *aesthetics*, such as our looks—and forget about personal values. The more we grow up, the more we might feel we need these 'goods' to satisfy our egos. Try and keep yourself in tune with your inner qualities by building from the inside out, not from the outside in.

Finally, we can learn about ourselves from *life experience*. For example, we might fail an exam or lose a job. In this case, doing better on the next exam or finding a new job can help us overcome failures and challenges through continued growth, learning and effort. Our appreciation of our innate qualities over time can be strengthened through success or difficulty, both of which come with life experience.

Altogether, there are at least four ways (described above) to strengthen appreciation of your inner qualities.

- Reflection
- Reminders from friends, family or other audience (i.e., seeing our positive impact on others)
- Engaging in rewarding activities
- Life experience

Overall, the greater our appreciation of our qualities, the greater our confidence to truly face life. Temporary sadness or other difficult emotions will arise, but your foundation will be the strongest it can be to go through these emotions.

INTERNAL COPING MECHANISMS

Do you have internal coping mechanisms that keep you going? Yes, life is challenging. Yes, you may face overwhelming difficulty. Yes, you may also get a big promotion. How do you cope with life as changes come and go? There are important habits that can keep you going when you may feel the blues. You may want to try some of these. (See *Tips to Elevate You When You Feel the Blues* or *Coping with Difficulty so that You Heal and Stay Healthy.)* You might use gratitude statements to keep you appreciative of the good, or you might benefit seeking help from a health professional. More than likely, you will be using a combination of mechanisms to keep you going.

Coping mechanisms help us feel strong emotionally and physically. These mechanisms help us filter away negative energy and channel our inner strength. Whether we go to the treadmill or to a trusted friend, we can build in routines that help bolster our sense of optimism, positivity, and overall well-being. Improved coping mechanisms can provide an optimistic outlook on life, which a Harvard study has linked to living significantly longer.[92]

When we may feel overwhelmed with emotion, self-expression can become extremely useful. If we don't have someone there to understand us, we may need to resort to coping strategies we can use on our own. We might further use exercise and diet to boost our heart and brain health. We might write down our thoughts, possibly so that others can benefit. We might pray and hope for the best, and then let life unravel as it may. We might learn to accept things as they are rather than becoming flustered by them. We might shift our attention or energy to others rather than ourselves. Again, more than likely, we will use a combination of mechanisms to keep us going.

Altogether, there are at least five helpful ways (mentioned above) that people might cope internally.

- Improve exercise and diet
- Write down your thoughts, for yourself or possibly for others to benefit
- Pray and hope for the best, then let life unravel as it may
- Learn to accept things as they are
- Shift attention or energy to others rather than ourselves

Not all internal coping will come naturally. Developing discipline to engage in these activities and more is important. Positive self-talk or "self-coaching" is also key to sustaining helpful coping. (See the article *5 Tips to Exude Confidence in Your Character* for more about positive self-talk.)

In sum, we ought to answer with confidence these two key questions: 1) How strong is your personal identity, or your appreciation of your inner qualities? 2) Do you have internal coping mechanisms that keep you going? If you can answer these questions with confidence and strength, you will likely navigate through life more easily when circumstances change. Keep strengthening your character, and you will eventually see and feel the impact your heart has on others.

(*The Huffington Post*, January 2017)

PART III

SELF-IMPROVEMENT

5 TIPS TO BUILD EMOTIONAL STRENGTH

Do you want to be more thick-skinned? Be less sensitive, perhaps? Question this: Can you foresee your circumstances tomorrow? Next month? Next year? How can you prepare, in advance, to go through life's ups and downs, with all the emotional highs and lows? Consider these five tips.

1. WHEN YOU ARE PRESENTED WITH A DIFFICULTY, LOOK FOR THE OPPORTUNITY TO FIGURE OUT WHAT THE CHALLENGE IS TELLING YOU, AND THE BEST NEXT STEPS TO TAKE.

Letting yourself face difficulty today could be necessary, so you can find the perspective and drive to live your life with greater enthusiasm tomorrow. With that in mind, sadness or a tough time might be more worth it than you thought, as hard as that may be to hear. Dr. Maya Angelou, American poet and civil rights activist, once said, "Life is not measured by the number of breaths we take, but by the moments that take our breath away." We move forward in life for the opportunity to have our next breath taken away. Not only do we crave to be excited, filled with joy, proud as ever, or in awe of another's spirit and impact; we wish it could happen all the time. Figuring out those next best steps to take after a down moment or after getting through a rough time can help you win another chance to have your breath taken away in time.

2. WORK TO FULFILL YOUR DREAMS, IN ORDER TO MAINTAIN SATISFACTION AND SUSTAIN MOTIVATION. KNOWING YOU ARE ON THE RIGHT TRACK CAN HELP YOU WAVER LESS IN THE FACE OF DIFFICULTY.

Do you have life goals, or dreams? Or are you going through the routine of life without considering what makes you especially satisfied? Consider this: Dr. Angelou said, "If one is lucky, a solitary fantasy can totally transform one million realities." Your emotional resilience feeds off of your passion and willpower. By working towards the right goals and dreams for you, your emotional strength can be invigorated repeatedly and often. From time to time, you may feel pressed, but your passion can keep you thick-skinned, while the right luck can help you transform others' realities.

3. IN TIMES OF DIFFICULTY, RELY ON OTHERS WHO KNOW YOU THE BEST, AND WHOSE SUPPORT MATTERS TO YOU.

While having faith in yourself matters tremendously, from time to time we may need reinforcement from those around us in order to continue persevering. Surrounding ourselves with positive, strong figures is critical—people whose support we can feel, and be genuinely motivated by.

4. GO EASY ON YOURSELF. LIFE CAN BE UNPREDICTABLE.

Going easy, or practicing self-compassion, is important, because we can't expect to always succeed at all that we do. Congratulating ourselves for effort might mean treating yourself to a spa adventure or a handful of flowers. Consider self-compassion a necessity when you feel stressed out, especially. Take time to care for yourself, and tell yourself that you do, often.

5. STAY HUMBLE IF YOU FEEL REWARDED OFTEN.

Celebrating success, yours and others', can be a great feeling. However, remember to stay humble if you are repeatedly rewarded perhaps with success, compliments, or money. Such rewards can be fleeting and temporary, so it might be wise to leave bragging behind should this apply to you. Hopefully, you are blessed with humility and success often. If so, try to help others as much as possible. Remember, as has been said before, "The best feeling is when you're happy because you've made somebody else happy."

Consider these five tips to building emotional strength in the face of struggles that you may face. Acknowledging and reminding yourself that everyone feels emotional ups and downs is wise; it can help you feel connected in times of difficulty, and can help remind you that you are human, which is important in maintaining humility. Remember to go easy on yourself, and continue to give yourself perspective and new steps to take.

(*The Huffington Post*, August 2017)

7 STEPS TO WORK ON YOUR SHORTCOMINGS

Do you have shortcomings? Are you interested in working on areas you could improve as a person? Where should you start? And what can you do?

Below are seven ways to work on your weakest area—whether it is being too critical, too sensitive, too argumentative, just too lazy, or something else.

1. THINK OF TWO OR THREE ASPECTS OF YOURSELF THAT YOU WANT TO WORK ON.

Perhaps by writing down your thoughts or having a conversation with a friend or loved one, you can start to jot down areas you would like to improve upon. Consider traits or habits that you might not be satisfied with, or that you feel are keeping you from success. Write these down somewhere.

2. BEGIN TO SUGGEST HOW OR WHY YOU DEVELOPED THE UNSATISFYING TRAITS OR HABITS.

It might be simply that you've always been this way, or it might be because you recently lost a loved one or encountered a tough circumstance. Beginning to frame the reasons for unsatisfying traits or habits will give you a deeper understanding of yourself and help you envision a direction for change.

3. REMIND YOURSELF THAT THERE'S ROOM FOR IMPROVEMENT, WHILE ACCEPTING THAT YOU FACE A SHORTCOMING.

Let's say you are too critical of others, and that dampens your relationships. In order to work on this less-satisfying trait, it is a good idea to tell yourself you can tweak your trait, while accepting that it might be hard for you.

4. BRAINSTORM WAYS TO WORK ON EACH SHORTCOMING.

Let's stick with being overly critical. You can begin to be less critical of others by brainstorming ways to develop more openness and understanding. Jot these down and try to make them fun and creative. Remember to keep with your vision of change, as mentioned in step two.

5. REPEAT STEPS OR WAYS TO REPLACE THE OLD TRAIT OR HABIT.

When you set out to change a shortcoming, you'll likely face resistance. Repeating the steps or ways to correct your shortcoming can help you sustain the willpower to continue improving. Soon, with training, you can begin to feel the old habits sliding away and your use of the newly desired trait settling in. It might take more effort to be less critical, for example, but over time and with practice, it will get easier.

6. GO EASY ON YOURSELF.

We all deserve more self-compassion. It can be easy to get caught up in dissatisfaction, and even frustration, with aspects you don't find fulfilling about yourself. As Oprah Winfrey said, however, "Nobody's journey is seamless or smooth. We all stumble. We all have setbacks. It's just life's way of saying, 'Time to change course.'" Remembering that each person's journey is difficult for them should give you the strength and perspective to promote self-compassion during your own journey.

7. TRY TO FOCUS AND HARNESS YOUR OWN STRENGTHS WHILE WORKING ON YOUR SHORTCOMINGS.

Instead of concerning yourself with the success or strengths of others, focus on building your own strengths in your spare time. Harness the power of what makes you feel good and lets you shine. This will make your shortcomings feel less intimidating and give you a sense that you're on the right path.

Remember: if you are able to work on your shortcomings instead of feeling cornered by them, you will likely feel more inspired and satisfied. Try these tips, and hopefully soon, you can harness your power to feel great and help others!

(*The Huffington Post*, August 2017)

4 WAYS TO GET TOUGHER THROUGH EXPERIENCE

Oftentimes we don't realize how our life experiences can make us tougher. Whether it's recovering from a bad day, moving on from an illness, or losing a relationship, here are four ways in which your experiences can make you tougher if you consider the following.

1. YOU LEARN TO EXPRESS YOURSELF.

When we face a difficulty, those with a social support system quickly find themselves expressing their worries, fears, and sources of stress. If you are without a trusted listener, you may use a therapist. Either way, when we learn to express our emotions honestly and freely, we feel much of our tension float away. This is very important. While some of us have learned to bottle up our emotions, the truth is that expressing yourself—at the right time and to the right person, if possible—can be tremendously relieving. This can leave you ready to face life anew.

2. YOU LEARN YOUR LIMITS.

In tough situations, we feel pressure that can place an unpleasant amount of stress on us. After realizing that we are only human and cannot take every source of stress, we find our limits. You can find ways to minimize the source of stress afterwards. For example, if you have a career that is not working out, you may want to find a hobby to keep you satisfied as much as possible. Then, in time, you might consider finding a new career that is your passion (or even possibly that hobby!).

3. YOU PLAY TO YOUR STRENGTHS.

All of us have a unique ability to shine in our own way. Look for this strength, and run with it. As Dr. Maya Angelou said, "I believe every person is born with talent," so play to your strength. If each of us learned to capitalize on our unique abilities to do good, move another, help another, lift another, there would be more goodness, joy, love, and peace in the world. By practicing our strengths, we gain confidence and self-esteem, and become tougher in what is likely a rewarding and uplifting way.

4. YOU WILL BOUNCE BACK STRONGER THE NEXT TIME.

The ability to "bounce back" from a bad mood, or a rough day, week, or year, ultimately comes down to a shift in thinking and supply of motivation. When you practice the habit of "bouncing back," you strengthen this habit and can ultimately sustain positive energy for longer periods of time. Practicing gratitude is one way to help with that shift in thinking. Life circumstances may change, and may not be optimal to one's choosing. Learning to come back stronger and quicker is perhaps one of the best ways to be toughened up, refining your resilience.

Keep in mind these four ways that experience will make you tougher, and you'll be more ready to achieve what you want. While there may be unexpected difficulties on the road, remember you can bounce back stronger next time.

(*The Huffington Post*, April 2017)

3 WAYS TO BE LESS HARD ON YOURSELF

Have you ever felt like you expect a lot from yourself? Are you not quite satisfied with your performance? Perhaps you want to consider being less hard on yourself. How? Try these three tips, and then sit back and see your satisfaction levels rise higher than before.

1. CONSIDER WHAT YOU WANT TO ACHIEVE NEXT AS A WORK IN PROGRESS. TAKE MEASURED STEPS TO GET THERE.

If you expect yourself to run a marathon after three gym visits, there's obviously a disconnect between expectation and realistic performance. If you take measured steps towards what you want to achieve next in your life—whether it be completing a degree, earning a promotion at your job, or actually running a marathon—you'll leave more cushion for detours that may come as a surprise. What that means is, you'll be prepared to wrestle with emotional ups and downs, potential challenges in your career, or even missed gym visits. You leave less room for disappointment this way.

Looking at your goals as a work in progress, but still aiming for success, can make your journey all that more comfortable and satisfying—and, it can make you less hard on yourself.

2. LOOK AT WHAT YOU HAVE ACHIEVED, AND OWN IT. Many overachievers can't acknowledge their successes, largely due to a preoccupation with what they desire next. When you are this hard on yourself, it's hard to own what you have accomplished. Consider your achievements as time very well-spent. Truly take a great amount of satisfaction and boost from that and you'll look forward with even greater confidence in yourself.

3. IF YOU GET KNOCKED DOWN, CONSIDER THERE COULD BE A REASON. LET YOURSELF GET BACK UP WITH CONFIDENCE AND A GREATER UNDERSTANDING OF WHAT HAPPENED.

We've all been knocked down in some form or another, some of us more than others. When this happens, consider that there might be a reason for the present challenge and don't get too frustrated. Let time take its course. Let yourself get back up with confidence and a greater understanding of what happened to knock you down, and subsequently charge your motivation further.

In the three above tips, you can learn to view your efforts towards a work in progress, own your achievements, and reflect thoughtfully when you get knocked down, all for the sake of being less hard on yourself. Hopefully, you will feel more satisfaction with the use of these!

(*The Huffington Post*, September 2017)

10 WAYS TO BE A BETTER YOU IN THE NEW YEAR

Hoping to make your next year the best yet? Here are ten ways to be a better you for the upcoming year.

1. BE YOUR OWN BEST FRIEND.

In order to put your best foot forward, try and ensure proper self-care. How? Manage your time so you get good nutrition, adequate rest, and anything else that can help you feel motivated and upbeat.

2. PLAN AHEAD.

Why does planning count? Planning can help you make the most of your time, either by working towards goals that you've thought of, or by setting aside time for a well-earned vacation. By investing now, you're more likely to reap positive returns later, both emotionally and physically.

3. STAY INVESTED.

When you feel like your resolutions or goals lack the needed effort, figure out what drives you so you'll stay invested in longer-term projects as well as personal and professional ambitions. If you're still searching for that ideal career, consider your skills and passion to make the optimal investment. (I have written about this in a separate article. See *3 Steps to Figure Out Your Ideal Career*.)

4. UPLIFT MORE.

Making a genuine effort to stay positive will feed into all aspects of your life. If you haven't already, try your hand at uplifting yourself by staying healthy, thinking optimistically, and feeling hopeful, and likely you'll have a positive impact on others while doing so.

5. WORK SMART.

Stay focused on your goals, both near- and long-term, in order to get the biggest return from your personal investment. If you're unsure how to "work smart," try to figure out your goals first, and next map out how you'll get there.

6. DON'T BE AFRAID TO ASK FOR HELP.

Many major endeavors require team effort. Asking for help is a sign of wisdom and not a sign of weakness. Asking frequently is a sign that you care—undoubtedly a positive trait. Without asking, you may get to a dead end quickly, so steer toward success by asking questions and often from those you trust.

7. STAY LOVING, AND OFTEN.

Stay loving, often, and you'll find frustration, worry and other pre-occupations can fade away quickly and naturally.

8. LEARN FROM OTHERS.

Trying to learn from others is not only a reflection of intelligence; it can reveal empathy and a willingness to build character, demonstrate open-mindedness, and support understanding. Stay open to learning, and success could soon follow.

9. STAY COURAGEOUS.

By persevering day-in and day-out, you are showing how courageous you can be. Keep channeling your courage by making a difference in your own life, first and foremost. Soon, you may positively impact others by reaching for your goals.

10. DO WHAT YOU DO BEST, AND OFTEN.

When you find a strength in your repertoire, make sure to channel and fine-tune it. Whether you're savvy at business or passionate at baking, building on your strengths will keep you busy and your time well-spent.

Above are ten ways to be a better you for the year to come. Hopefully, the upcoming year will be filled with more success, both personally and professionally, as ever yet!

(*The Huffington Post*, January 2018)

5 IDEAS ON HOW TO CREATE OPTIMISM

A sense of optimism may reduce our risk from dying from major causes, including heart-related disease, according to a recent Harvard study of 70,000 women.[93] *According to Dr. Travis Bradberry, the foremost leader in emotional intelligence research, we should not only tell ourselves the best is yet to come; we should believe it.*

Here are five ways, in these uncertain times, we can improve our optimistic outlook.

1. WRITE DOWN SPECIFIC OUTCOMES THAT CAN HAPPEN IN YOUR LIFE—IN TERMS OF CAREER, FAMILY, OR FRIENDSHIPS—IN A FORWARD-LOOKING PERSONAL REFLECTION.

Postdoctoral research fellow Kaitlin Hagan, co-lead author of the Harvard study, describes this forward-looking step as a low-cost, and likely useful, intervention. For example, you might consider yourself becoming a gracious host for family and friend parties in a few years.

2. EXERCISE ROUTINELY AND DON'T HESITATE TO SHARE YOUR WORKOUT ACHIEVEMENTS WITH OTHERS.

Regular exercise has numerous health benefits, including strengthened immune system, stronger joints, better sleeping quality, improved blood sugar levels, reduced risk of heart disease and more.[94] Running, hiking, or yoga are examples of exercises that may protect you from feelings of anxiousness or "the blues." You may even choose to join an exercise group online that meets regularly, or work out with a friend or family member.

3. FIND WHAT YOU ARE PASSIONATE ABOUT, AND MOVE FORWARD ON THAT!

According to author Ayo Olaniyan, who writes on how to build optimism, embarking on a journey with a purpose will keep you feeling more optimistic than if you just went through the motions.[95] For example, you might be an especially good listener and decide to pursue a graduate degree in social work or counseling. Whatever your interest, make sure to work consistently at it, hone your skills, and build on your goals.

If you are having trouble identifying your ideal career or skill sets, see the article entitled *3 Steps to Figure Out Your Ideal Career.*

4. REMEMBER, THERE ARE FAILURES ON THE PATH TO SUCCESS.

Accept these as part of the process. According to Dr. Travis Bradberry, highly successful people are resilient to failure while pursuing success. In a recent study at the College of William and Mary, researchers interviewed 800 entrepreneurs and found that the most successful were "terrible at imagining failure."[96] So, while you may have been fired from or quit a job, remember: the opportunity to pursue your passion and succeed in fulfilling your potential may be next on the path to larger success. Failures are part of the process.

5. CELEBRATE OTHER PEOPLE'S SUCCESS.

If you cannot be happy for others' success, take it as a signal that your own life's outlook may need some polishing. You may not be happy for every success outside of your closest social networks, but at least work on adopting the mindset for friends and family. You may see a deeper optimism rise in you.

In total, you can try these ways to help improve your sense of optimism. Instilling this sense in ourselves has many health benefits and can help you find happiness, success, and satisfaction in the long run. From the ways suggested above, pick the ones that can help you create a powerful optimistic view in your life.

(*The Huffington Post*, January 2017)

CONQUERING YOUR FEARS WHEN THEY GET IN THE WAY OF YOUR SUCCESS—PART I

How often do you find yourself facing fear? Fear of failure, the future, a painful memory, your environment—and you can't seem to shake it off? You may be thinking: The struggle is real. Whether you're facing a difficult day, month, year, or set of years, conquering your fears may seem daunting or impossible.

Being stuck in such a set of circumstances, however, is certainly not where your strength ends. Here are five tips to conquering and asserting yourself over those fears that grab hold and scare you when you're feeling vulnerable.

1. DON'T UNDERESTIMATE THE POWER OF CORRECTIVE THINKING.

In other words, put your fears into perspective. Ask yourself first, why does that fear bother you in the first place? Because you'd rather focus on the positive—you can do better than that, but *you are human.* Try to remember that positive emotions of appreciation and acceptance are on the flip side of your momentary fear, and gradually allow yourself to focus on the positive thoughts. For example, financial setbacks might have some worried of losing a home and becoming homeless. Pretty scary, no? Remember, in the face of financial setbacks, you may still have your loved ones (family or friends), and basking in all that love can keep you appreciative and strong. Another example is if you're fearful of not being able to pass an exam. Pulling an all-nighter? Avoiding studying? Try to stay calm, breathe and focus on the fact that you're trying to learn. You care. Once you've applied corrective thinking, fearful thoughts can dissipate. You can try writing down statements that reflect your corrective thinking as well.

2. REMEMBER THAT THE NEXT DAY WILL COME.

You have plenty of chances to fill your days with joy, especially with the will to keep plugging away in your life journey. Perhaps try waking up at dawn to remind yourself of the beauty that lies in the start of a new day. Your hope and perseverance can drive you to find new shades of meaning such as what "grit" means or discovering a new sense of appreciation in the face of hardship. Appreciation often comes with relief. Tell yourself: "My better days are ahead."

3. TRAIN YOURSELF TO USE SOOTHING MENTAL IMAGERY WHEN YOU FACE A CHALLENGING FEAR.

For example, if you're afraid of needles, imagine putting that fear into a leaf on a pond. Imagine water drops from another leaf dripping slowly into the leaf carrying your fear, with the negativity-filled leaf drifting away ever so slowly on the pond. Repeat this for an extra soothing effect.

4. REMIND YOURSELF THAT YOU ARE TRYING YOUR BEST AND THAT'S WHAT MATTERS.

Remembering that fears do not define you can often challenge what feels like backpedaling and condition powerful thoughts of goodness and strength in your persona. Tell yourself you are trying your best and that's what matters.

5. REMEMBER THE POWER OF PRAYER.

Of course, all our prayers may not come through to our satisfaction as quickly as we may want, so use this piece of advice while maintaining realistic expectations and lots of hope. Prayer can help you find hope, and hope can help you feel comforted. If this doesn't seem to do the trick, remember your perseverance in the face of great fear or challenge is a testament to your audacity and strength. Your courage grows every night you close your eyes to fall asleep and every morning your soul rises to a new day. This is the deepest form of courage.

Remember, you are always moving forward in your journey, which in itself is the most beautiful act.

(*The Huffington Post*, May 2016)

CONQUERING YOUR FEARS WHEN THEY GET IN THE WAY OF YOUR SUCCESS—PART II

The struggle is real when facing a difficult emotion such as fear in our lives. But remember these four things—you are not alone; expressing your difficulty will help you find relief; allowing time to heal is important, so be patient; and channeling difficult emotions into positive habits or hobbies can be extremely helpful.

So, consider the upside to these four very important tips to help you alleviate your fears.

1. REMEMBER, YOU ARE NOT ALONE.

You are in the company of many others. Putting this piece in perspective will help you feel more human and less frustrated, hopefully, in times of difficulty. You may even be aware of others who face similar conditions to yours. While it is hard to feel like your fears are keeping you tense, worried, or uncertain, the truth is that the feeling of fear is felt in excess across billions of people in the world. Not a single person has gone without feeling fear.

Is that good enough though? You might be thinking: "It's so debilitating!" or "I can't wait for happier times, success, and for my worries to all disappear!"

Your struggle is personal. It *is* hard. It causes overwhelming emotions. But, it can become unquestionably easier if you have a person to share your thoughts with and who hears your pain.

2. SO DON'T KEEP IT INSIDE. EXPRESS YOURSELF TO A TRUSTED RELATIVE, LOVED ONE, OR PROFESSIONAL, AND YOU'LL FIND IMMEDIATE AND LONG-TERM RELIEF. SELF-EXPRESSION IS VITAL.

Whether sharing with a healthcare professional, a family member, or a friend, sharing what is on your mind with someone who has time to care for you can be very important. Be honest with the person you are confiding in, express yourself to your level of comfort, and be honest with yourself about which fears are the hardest to face in your time of difficulty. Worry, anxiousness, anger, grief, and sadness can all be underlying sources of fear. Watch them slowly be lifted from your mindset, and soon (while it may take time) you will triumph. Make sure you trust the person you talk to; that you feel as comfortable and open with them as possible; and that you respect their feedback.

3. LETTING TIME HEAL CAN BE A POWERFUL APPROACH TO ANY OBSTACLE YOU FACE.

This will certainly help. While we may be impatient, and this tip may seem unhelpful at first, remember: long-term patience is vital. In the meantime, use the other coping mechanisms mentioned below. Don't underestimate the impact that passing time can have. Life is a roller coaster of emotions. With the right bag of coping skills, you will see the ups eventually outweigh the downs. Allow time to soothe your emotions and let you triumph over your fears, grief, and other difficulties.

4. CHANNEL YOUR FEARS OR NEGATIVITY INTO POSITIVE HABITS AND HOBBIES.

Everyone has unique interests, so make sure you have time to enjoy your passions, whether they are exercise (e.g., running, swimming, yoga), music, art, meditation, or any other fun interest. We often enjoy our lives more with a positive habit or hobby that shows we are pampering ourselves away from difficulty and into good times. So, make sure to care for yourself with positive habits and hobbies. You can even share the good times with a loved one or friend!

So, while the struggle may be very real, the rewards of the following nine tips, shared below, will help you celebrate the good times in the midst of difficulty. Seem unlikely? Try them out!

1. Use the power of corrective thinking.
2. Remember that the next day will come.
3. Remember to use soothing mental imagery when you might be facing a negative thought.
4. Remind yourself of the good person that you are and can be.
5. Remember the power of prayer.
6. Remember you are not alone.
7. Express your difficulties to someone you trust and respect.
8. Allow time to heal your difficulties.

9. Channel your fears or negativity into positive habits and hobbies to make you feel successful and accomplished.

(*The Huffington Post*, May 2016)

WHY BEING GOOD ISN'T ENOUGH AND GETTING BETTER IS THE MORE SUCCESSFUL MINDSET

When you're stuck in a bad mood, facing a challenge, or lacking confidence in your ability to accomplish a task, how do you react? Is your automatic reaction to think, "I'm just not able to do this. I don't have it in me"? Or, do you react by thinking, "I can get better at this if I work at it"?

The truth is, according to social psychologists, that most of us feel we don't have the innate ability to do certain things, but that's *not the way it works.*

Social psychology, and specifically Dr. Heidi Grant Halvorson, describe "incremental theorists" as the group of people who feel they can "get better" at practically any task or skill they apply themselves to.

This is in contrast to "entity theorists," who believe they have a fixed amount or type of, say, intelligence or personality. These folks want to just "be good," and must routinely be validated to prove they have "it"—be that intelligence, personality, etc.—or else they feel rejected.

What is the overarching difference between the two types? One, according to social psychology, is better for you; and the other will make you feel like you'll never have enough.

Let's take Roger Federer, a star sports athlete and the GOAT of the sport of tennis. Many critics have said he couldn't last as successfully as he has in the sport at a later age; that his age would limit him. What did Federer do? He has kept his personal and professional lives balanced and successful to the point where he was "getting better with age" in the sport in his mid- to late-thirties.[97] Athletes like Federer often make comebacks, bounce back, and use their "get better" mindset to defy the status quo.

So what can we learn from Federer? That "getting better" is an art form in itself. The mindset is key. Attitude is key. The ability to maneuver difficulty and challenges, tagged with giving yourself permission to feel down, stay patient, and be ready to seize the next opportunity when things don't work your way, is quite valuable and even indispensable.

The ability to move forward through the ups and downs comes with effort and experience. Amassing a network of support, friendships, respect, and love for what you do is also key. Federer himself points to his friends, family, and coaching team as a big part of his success.[98] Together, they're part of what makes the magic of "getting better" the more rewarding mindset.

Ultimately, the mindset of "getting better" is more beneficial than just your common "be good" attitude in terms of receiving lasting success, satisfaction and happiness. Hopefully, you will find the ways to achieve a more successful "get better" mindset now.

(*GratCircle.com*, February 2019)

5 PATHS TO POSITIVE CHARACTER FLOW

In business, positive cash flow is the basic concept of having a flow of money (income) that is higher than the outflow (expenses). Positive cash flow is, of course, necessary for a profitable and successful business.

In everyday living, though, the way we conduct "business" in terms of relationships, both personal and professional, is less black-and-white than positive cash flow. Say you have experience in marketing and a friend asks you for help with advertising an idea. Would you make time to help them? Or do you save all your expertise for paying clients?

There is another type of flow we should pay attention to as we find success—a reversed flow that comes from appreciating what is valuable in life. I call this "positive character flow," and it is characterized by giving more than we take.

Successful entrepreneurs are guided in their decision-making by positive cash flow as well as positive character flow. The value an entrepreneur sees in others and others' assets often strengthens cash flow and character flow.

Here are five gifts you can give, and appreciate in others, in order to promote both positive cash flow and positive character flow.

1. GIVING TIME

In business, a company's assets reflect its cumulative financial holdings, including cash, inventory, land, etc. One of an entrepreneur's assets is time. By appreciating others' time—and sharing their own—entrepreneurs can recognize and develop significant character. For example, say a volunteer position requires a two-hundred-hour time commitment. The investment is valuable because it reveals one's interests and willingness to give of their time. In return, the commitment itself develops the volunteer's character, i.e., positive character flow.

2. SHARING CONNECTIONS

Connections often help us succeed in business and in life. Valuing connections is extremely important to junior entrepreneurs seeking to build a business. A great example is the show *Shark Tank*, in which the top prize is connection to a billionaire who has other strategic connections. When a successful entrepreneur gives from another of their assets, namely professional connections, character flow is built. Sharing connections, whether with colleagues, family, or friends, can help shape meaningful relationships. At times, financial rewards are gained by giving or sharing one's connections, like for the Sharks.

3. OFFERING EXPERTISE

Expertise is an asset developed both in business and in life (as wisdom). With success comes an opportunity to pay it forward, which certainly builds character flow. A published author, for example, might help a novice understand the process of publishing a book. Or perhaps an experienced family member helps you negotiate the terms of a professional contract. It's critical to value others' expertise to overcome bottlenecks along a business path.

4. A WILLINGNESS TO HELP

If you're in search of a job, you're likely looking for a desired monetary benefit and/or experience. You sell your education, job history, and skills on your résumé. Your competency is on display, but recruiters are looking for how hard you're willing to work. They want to see your willingness to help with things big and small. A person who is willing to help understands the intangible satisfaction of giving back to others, which makes them a believer in positive character flow.

5. MAKING OTHERS FEEL GOOD

The biggest pillar, perhaps, in attaining positive character flow in life is rooted in how we make others feel. If we do not show we care, others may feel neglected and ignored, despite our intentions. As a volunteer crisis counselor for Crisis Text Line, I understand the importance of allowing others to feel heard and valued. Such help lines exist to allow those in need to feel heard.

Helping others to feel supported, cared for, valued, and appreciated is tremendously vital to a life worth living. Positive character flow is achieved regularly through this last gift. The way we make others feel reflects our appreciation of humanity, decency and goodness. If you are a new or successful entrepreneur, giving back to others—whether personally or professionally—is particularly meaningful. Why? Relationships are strengthened when others are remembered, acknowledged, and valued. As psychologist and philosopher William James once said, "The deepest craving of human nature is the need to be appreciated."

At the end of the day, both positive character flow and positive cash flow are ingredients to feeling content and satisfied. Learning to appreciate the five gifts above can help bring tangible and intangible rewards, and ultimately success in both business and in life.

(*Entrepreneur Magazine*, December 2020)

PART IV

ESTABLISHING CAREER PATHS AND GOAL-SETTING

3 STEPS TO FIGURE OUT YOUR IDEAL CAREER

Are you unsure of what career you really want? Do you want a career that will truly make you happy? Follow these three steps, and perhaps your ideal career will land itself in front of you!

1. SKILL SETS

First, ask yourself: What are your biggest skill sets? Have you worked on previous projects that were successful? If so, what did you contribute? How were you helpful? Perhaps you were good at the research needed or the writing involved. Maybe you were an effective public speaker, or a natural performer. Whatever the skills may have been, review your past contributions to previous projects, internships, or jobs to find two or three prominent skills that you have demonstrated successfully and repeatedly.

If you have not been involved in many previous endeavors, find various projects to attempt (be they internships or volunteer work), and see what you're good at. Sometimes a school setting can reveal your skill sets, but I suggest being engaged in actual tangible commitments to find your true skills. It may even be a natural talent you have, such as, say, being artistic.

2. PASSION

Second, consider what you always wanted to do—something that you hold a passion for, but may have thought too difficult. Some might say that whatever the field, unless you feel completely confident in it, don't do it. I say challenge yourself. The field that you have a passion for—maybe it is dance, or inspirational speaking—but find challenging will always push you to strive to be better.

You may not be perfect at it now, but this is why you're choosing a career in it: in order to *feel* successful. Maybe it is singing, or writing bestselling fiction stories. Think about what will just make you the happiest.

3. YOUR PERFECT (YET PRACTICAL) CAREER

Third, combine your skill sets with your passion to find that perfect, yet practical, career. The reason it is likely practical for you is because you have already demonstrated success in the skills needed to achieve an even more successful, longer-term career, through previous projects, internships, etc. The reason it is likely perfect for you, well, is because you'll likely always be passionate about it and want to improve at it day after day. Maybe your ideal career is being an environmental engineer, or a movie actor.

Let me give you just one example of how to apply this formula.

First, let's say, you have shown to be a natural in the subject of chemistry. Your knowledge or study of the field landed you a successful summer internship in a chemistry lab. You know you are also good with directions. This may not have landed you an internship, per se, but friends and family have repeatedly counted on your knack for directions to help get them to their destination.

Second, you are passionate about urban studies. You feel somewhat uncertain about how much of a natural you are at absorbing everything there is to urban studies, but you are passionate about making a difference in city landscapes around the U.S. or even around the world. Since you were young, perhaps you have dreamt of shaping city skylines or being famous for applying conservation principles to urban landscapes.

Now, third, put together your skill sets (chemistry knowledge and being good at directions) with your passion (urban studies or design), and you can determine that your dream job is an environmental engineer! You might now consider additional—and worthwhile—education you could pursue to specialize even further. You may be glad to know that your field pays especially well. You certainly can trust that you have picked a career in which you will most likely be happy and successful. (Likely, whenever you find a specialized field—the perks of knowing what you truly want!—the pay is likely higher as well, an added bonus.)

So, I suggest you try this with your skill sets and passions, and soon you will be well on your way to being even more successful!

(*The Huffington Post*, July 2016)

TWO WAYS TO COMPLETE YOUR LIFESTYLE AND CAREER

Will you be completely satisfied with an ideal career in the long term? I argue no. Even if you have the perfect career, there can be days when you feel a void. How you prepare to fill the void and feel satisfied begins with you. Here are two suggestions to make you even happier.

1. INCORPORATE HOBBIES INTO YOUR ROUTINE. Whether this is exercise, modeling, acting, singing, or other ways of getting creative, the hobbies in your life will help you feel like you are treating yourself well. I consider this "pampering" and it is important to maintaining self-care; if you have always wanted to bake, but your career is eating away at your time, all the more reason to pursue baking as a hobby. I suggest pursuing at least two other hobbies outside of work or your regular routine.

Once you determine at least two hobbies that you've always had a passion for and that make you feel good, schedule time at least once a week to actively enjoy them.

2. FIND WAYS TO GENERATE MULTIPLE STREAMS OF INCOME.

Oftentimes, relying on a single income adds risk should economic conditions turn stark. I suggest figuring out what else you like to do and are good at (i.e., your skill sets), and find ways to generate at least one stream of additional income. If you need to know where to start, think about what you have repeatedly been successful at to find your skill sets (e.g., blogging, singing, software coding, graphic design, etc.) and then consider who you need to contact to develop a working, financially lucrative relationship. Multiple incomes can protect you from financial instability and can help you make use of the many interests you have.

The "side hustle" is quite common, but may not necessarily utilize your skills sets. An *Entrepreneur Magazine* article cites fifty "profitable" side hustles, ranging from selling items on Ebay or Craigslist to managing social media for a small business.[99] Other side hustles include: getting a part-time job, writing an ebook, creating YouTube tutorials, selling products on Etsy, or starting a food truck. If your side hustle utilizes your skill sets, all the better. If not, still being able generate additional streams of income can help support your financial security and peace of mind.

So, in order to begin leading a more balanced, and financially-secure lifestyle, try to do these two things: 1. Incorporate hobbies into your lifestyle (e.g., exercise, knitting, modeling, writing, painting, real estate work, hiking, yoga, gardening, etc.), and 2. Find ways to generate multiple streams of income.

(*The Huffington Post*, August 2016)

3 TRAITS NEEDED TO ACHIEVE YOUR GOALS

For most of us, the act of actually understanding, writing down, and actively working towards our goals has little place in our daily schedule. At the same time, many of us often feel stuck—like we can't get to that next job, that next achievement or relationship, or that next phase in life that we believe we should move into to feel happier. Yet, we do not seem to act on what we want. What qualities generate the willpower and the motivation to successfully move towards your goals? If you can muster these three strengths, maintain them in your repertoire, and effectively use them in achieving your goals, you could be very happy.

1. RESILIENCE

The ability to know when to adjust, fine-tune, or even completely change a goal, and *to not be discouraged* when that happens, is very important. For example, if you feel unsuccessful in finding a new job that you desire, you can try to pause for a couple of weeks or months and learn more about yourself and your strengths and weaknesses in the process. Then, after some time, rather than idly applying for random jobs that are not in your sweet spot, you will be applying with greater motivation to jobs that you are more qualified for. This also requires the ability to know your professional strengths and weaknesses—which brings me to the second strength you need.

2. INTROSPECTIVENESS

The ability to gauge what you are good at, what your passions are, and ultimately what can make you even happier (while hopefully remaining grateful and satisfied in the present) is a very strong trait to have. Some of us have this innate ability. Others could learn to be more introspective. The value of being successfully introspective can help in many ways. For example, if you want to build a positive attitude, you can begin by learning what you like about your personal traits. Learning to self-value your best traits is critical to projecting confidence, maintaining a positive attitude, and gaining self-respect. A positive attitude also comes from doing things that make you happy—hobbies such as art, music, sports, or cooking. When engaged in doing uplifting activities that we enjoy, we can often gain self-esteem and strengthen our positive attitude. However, we may not always feel uplifted or positive every single moment—which brings me to the third strength you need.

3. PERSEVERANCE

The ability to keep actively working on goals that you set and reset in spite of feeling down at times will keep you successful in the long term, no doubt. When in pursuit of things that are very important to us—such as a job we love, a life partner we love, or our continued health—we must be willing to be patient. As the proverb goes, "The best things in life come to those who wait." Of course, there must be effort invested in the waiting process. Patience is expected during the journey. Ultimately, the bigger goals with respect to our careers, spouses, and securing our health and happiness may seem to come slowly, but hopefully these goals are the most rewarding of them all.

With these three strengths—resilience, introspectiveness, and perseverance—you can make significant gains while working towards your goals. Meanwhile, as a goal-oriented individual, you can begin to feel like you're charting your own path and helping yourself realize your desires.

(*The Huffington Post*, August 2017)

3 REASONS TO REACH FOR HIGHER GOALS

Are you searching to make a bigger, more positive impact on yourself or possibly others? Do you feel like you're ready for a change in a bigger and better direction?

If you answered "yes" to either question, perhaps you're interested in reaching for higher goals to fulfill your ambitions. Here are three reasons you might want to reach for higher goals.

1. SEIZING BIGGER OPPORTUNITIES WILL LET YOU SHINE EVEN MORE.

When you're ready to make the leap to your next big project—whether it is writing a cookbook, starting a blog, or running a marathon—you are letting yourself shine even brighter. The decision to embark on a more time-consuming goal comes from internal ambition. You'll know when you're ready by how passionate you feel about taking the next step forward.

2. THE REWARDS COULD BE WORTH THE RISK.

A new commitment, such as writing a cookbook, could involve risks, like the amount of money and time invested. Consider this: Are the rewards even greater? If the answer is "yes," then you could be assured that the new venture might just be worth undertaking. You might just be a world-class chef that needs to take that next leap towards further success. If the answer is "no," then look for another project that will let you reap its rewards.

3. YOU ARE READY AND WILLING TO CONTINUE LEARNING IN ORDER TO CARRY OUT YOUR NEW VENTURE.

While a change in your goals might require more time, energy, money, and patience, one of the key aspects to this success will be your enthusiasm to keep learning. If you want to make a difference and can keep gaining knowledge from books and articles in your field of interest, then soon your passion can turn into success. It can get difficult at times to press onward. However, actually maintaining interest is half the effort.

Do you feel now that you're ready to reach for higher goals? Perhaps with a little bit of luck, success will come knocking on your door.

(*The Huffington Post*, October 2017)

HOW TO COMMIT TO REACHING A GOAL

Do you have plans for the future, or possibly a personal, professional, or other specific goal for yourself?
If not, have you ever thought about setting one? If so, are you on the right track to reaching your goal?

Here are four ways to commit yourself to reaching a goal.

1. BRAINSTORM

Perhaps your wish is for a higher salary, or an ideal family and marriage, or another future aspiration. What do you do when it seems like the ambition or goal is out of reach? Brainstorm. Try to come up with ideas to achieve your goal that others may not have thought of. For example, if your goal is to get a higher salary or raise, then consider setting a performance review meeting with your boss. The drive required to initiate such a meeting might be appreciated, and you could even be rewarded. It's important to brainstorm ideas and jot them down if your goals seem slightly out of reach. Then, it's time to get creative.

2. BE CREATIVE

When you're planning how to reach a goal, good thinking requires creativity. Think outside of the box. Also, remember this: the best ideas may be the most obvious and simple—ideas that make you wonder why no one else has thought of them yet. For example, previous changes made to Diet Coke include five new flavors, which promote their business goals. An idea like this could be a winning lottery ticket, simply because you had the creativity to come up with it. Next comes the hard work.

3. WORK HARD AND SMART

Nothing beats productivity, especially when you think you're on the right track to reaching a bigger goal. Working hard is oh-so-important to reaching a goal or bringing a plan to fruition. Embedded within this step is also the important action of working smart. A good example of working smart is asking for help from others, getting opinions, and incorporating feedback. Remember to work hard, work smart, and utilize all your resources.

4. STAY FOCUSED

Keeping your eye on the target is key. If you have a goal that is bigger, staying focused is even more important. Let's say you want to start a small business. In order to focus, think of the single most important element that will drive the success of your business. It could be the product or service you're selling, for example. Then, consistently improve this element to exponentially increase sales or expand your customer base. Keeping your focus on the service or product will lay the foundation of success and ultimately help you reach bigger goals.

So when you have trouble committing to a goal, remember there is much to gain by brainstorming, being creative, working hard and smart, and staying focused. You'll likely reach your objective by applying these four steps.

(*GratCircle.com*, February 2018)

HERE'S HOW TO PLAN BIG TO "MAKE IT BIG"

Have you considered making goals and actively working towards them besides your New Year's resolutions? You will be far ahead of most everyone else if you plan big to "make it big." In order to plan big, according to popular websites such as MindTools.com, you will need to follow three simple steps.

1. CONSIDER THE BIGGER PICTURE

First, think about where you want to be in the next ten years in broader categories, including financial status, family status, attitude, physical status, and career status (described by MindTools.com). Do you want to be a parent? Do you want to make over a $50k salary? Do you want to pamper yourself more? Pausing to reflect on where you want to end up in ten years will give you a long-term perspective that you will need initially in order to set goals for yourself.

2. SET INCREASINGLY SMALLER GOALS FOR YOURSELF

After putting your future plans in sight, begin to describe ten-year, five-year, yearly, monthly, weekly, and daily goals for yourself. If you want to increase your salary to over $70k in ten years, begin by setting one overarching goal (i.e., ten-year goal) and then increasingly smaller goals over the next five years, one year, months, weeks, and days. A monthly career goal might end up being to network with ten professionals in your field per month through LinkedIn posts, phone calls, in-person meetings, or via Skype. A weekly goal intended to improve physical status could be to go on two to three outdoor walks with a friend each week. Then, after charting your plans, you end up with daily, measurable goals that you can work toward.

3. WORK ACTIVELY TOWARD YOUR GOALS

Finally, you will want to put consistent effort towards your goals. While this may seem repetitive, you will still gain a sense of achievement at the end of each day, and you will sometimes be rewarded with new information and opportunities. For example, your daily financial goal could involve networking by emailing, calling, or LinkedIn messaging five contacts per day to find the job that satisfies your financial goals. By knowing you are hitting your targets, your efforts will make you feel successful at the end of each day, week, month or year. Ultimately, you are more likely to see the fruits of your labor rewarded than if you had not set goals for yourself in the first place.

So, consider these steps in setting goals for yourself, and you could definitely "make it big" by planning big!

(*The Huffington Post*, August 2016)

PART V

RELATIONSHIPS

WHY WE RISE BY LIFTING OTHERS

Have you ever actually stopped and thought about how someone else made you feel in a specific moment? Did you leave them feeling uplifted or happier?

When a person you love or care for opens a door to a brighter, more uplifting emotion, they often invite you to feel a certain way. We hold a door open for them when we are brave enough to see past ourselves. We hold a door open for them when we seek past ourselves in search of higher ground; that is, in search of helping another. We hold that door open for them when we sacrifice greed and ego for love, joy, shared happiness, and respect. When we hold that door open, our human condition is spared from a primal base and rather buttressed to a higher level. We become stronger; we become nobler; we become wiser—oftentimes without knowing it. Our own condition becomes fortified with dignity while another's is graced. The self-respect and mutual respect we gain from treating our relationships as if they are another chance to uplift one another is immeasurable.

Why is it that we rise by lifting others? It's complicated, to say the least. However, the sacrifice of ego that we make and the strengthening of love that we receive each are, indeed, a part of the beauty of the human condition.

(*GratCircle.com*, February 2019)

3 WAYS TO GIVE OUT OF THAT WHICH YOU LOVE

What are things you love for yourself? Money? Power? Has it ever occurred to you to give back things you love for yourself? Maybe at one point or another, you have considered donating money or other material goods. What about donating good values? Kindness, friendship, love, joy, and happiness, for example. If each of us were to spread just one such value, consider how much goodness and positivity it would generate. What are some of the values that you appreciate? Ask yourself: how could you help improve your immediate environment?

Below, I share three ways you could give out of that which you love.

1. GIVE BACK THROUGH YOUR BEST QUALITIES.

Your character is unique as your appearance. After you figure out your character strengths, figure out how to hone those strengths through specific and repeated actions. Such skill sets will be your voice to the world, letting you channel your greatness.

Think about what makes you so unique. Perhaps you are funny, so you might attempt to tell a joke every day to make someone laugh; or perhaps you are organized, and you might help your close friend reorganize their kitchen. Whatever your strength, work toward improvement and repeated action in order to deliver your talent to those around you.

2. SHARE YOUR APPRECIATION WITH OTHERS.

Wouldn't you love to feel appreciated? So, why not share your own appreciation?

Gratitude is a way to express the impact others can have on you. When you tell someone you appreciate them, or something specific they've done, you are opening the door to better-quality relationships and enduring love and kindness. Think about the supportive, encouraging, and positive people in your life. Then, share your appreciation of those people by sending a thank-you text, social media post, or a handwritten note. You will open the door to a great amount of positivity that can leave you feeling great.

3. PRACTICE A SMALL GESTURE OF KINDNESS, WHENEVER YOU HAVE THE OPPORTUNITY.

Small acts of kindness can help improve our mood, bring a smile to our face, or, better yet, make our day. And who doesn't love feeling better or happier?

Holding a door open for someone, smiling at a familiar face, asking someone how they are doing that day, or simply listening to their response and acknowledging their feelings—these are some of the small gestures of kindness that can bring light into others' lives when they might need it most. Consider bringing this positivity to your everyday routine. You will feel uplifted, happier, and more connected to your community.

In all, these are three ways you might give out of that which you love. Think about the next time you could give back through your qualities, be appreciative, or simply practice a kind gesture. More likely than not, you will feel the love in return.

(*The Huffington Post*, June 2017)

5 TIPS TO STRENGTHEN YOUR RELATIONSHIPS

What's the secret to happiness? According to the longest study on the topic, it's your relationships.

Harvard researchers examined a cohort of men for seventy-five years and found that their relationships were the number-one predictor of health and happiness. It wasn't about *how many* relationships a person had; rather, it was the *quality* that mattered.[100]

Each relationship has its ups and downs. Maintaining a relationship, whether it be romantic or platonic, requires work and perseverance.

Outside the Harvard study, here are a few tips to keep those relationships and bonds strong.

1. DON'T BE QUICK TO JUDGE.

Certainly, none of us can imagine the roads others have traveled to get to where they are, so don't assume you know what others think or feel. While first impressions may be important, remember: some relationships develop over time. Instead of judging, parse out your thinking to remember the good in others and you'll find yourself able to look at the upside of things more often. Always lend a friendly ear and stay considerate of others' feelings.

2. BE UNDERSTANDING.

Everyone might be busy, but most people could use a person who genuinely listens and does not undermine their feelings. This is the most valuable skill you could develop, and it will help you build the quality of your relationships.

3. REMEMBER: PEOPLE ARE BUSY.

Everyone has their own set of issues to deal with. They may be busy and preoccupied with their own lives. Be respectful of others' personal time, and share time with them when the opportunity arises. It may not be as often as you like, but it's important to be considerate of others' personal space.

4. AVOID GOSSIP.

Gossip can damage your relationships, self-worth, and it can also cause drama. Try not to gossip if you can even while sometimes people see this as a form of stress relief. Telling stories about others and giving opinions is one thing, but ruining someone else's reputation could come back to haunt you. Apply the golden rule you learned back in elementary school: Treat others the way you want to be treated!

5. STAY TRUE TO YOURSELF.

Building relationships takes understanding and support; however, that doesn't mean you should change yourself so others will like you more. Keep the qualities that make your character strong. Build on them, and don't let others make you compromise your values.

Each person you meet could potentially strengthen your network of family, friends, and acquaintances. Finding the people you feel good relating to can build satisfaction, which is vital to health and happiness.

Remember to be kind, thoughtful, caring, and truly considerate. Soon, you will gain the trust of others, and a lot of love, support, and *happiness* will find you.

(*The Huffington Post*, April 2016)

5 TIPS TO BE MORE UNDERSTANDING

Do you want to be understood—your feelings, circumstances, and point of view, for example? Do you make an effort to understand other people, even your closest friends? Most people, while wanting to be understood, do not simply have the time or energy to listen closely, really empathize, and attempt to understand one another. Yet, innately, we each desire to truly feel understood.

Why is it that while we want to feel understood, the ability to understand one another is so challenging?

Here are some tips to create more understanding in our lives, especially for those who we care about.

1. ASSUME THE LEAST ABOUT THE OTHER PERSON, RESERVING YOUR JUDGMENT AS MUCH AS POSSIBLE, WHILE SHOWING GENUINE EMPATHY.

"Our days are happier when we give people a piece of our heart rather than a piece of our mind." This quote summarizes how empathy and understanding can bring satisfaction to us while providing comfort to others. This cycle of satisfaction and comfort can also prevent and solve many problems in our social lives. Appreciating our differences in opinion, meanwhile, is a building block to understanding one another.

2. TRY TO LISTEN TO UNDERSTAND, RATHER THAN LISTENING TO REPLY.

"The biggest communication problem is that we do not listen to understand. We listen to reply," said educator Dr. Stephen Covey. It is okay if we fail to understand, but have the courage to reply, "I don't know to how to reply to that. That sounds tough." It's better to face the truth instead of replying without showing understanding.

Consider friends and family. We might not have an answer for why someone could be feeling frustrated, angry, or upset. The wisest thing to do, according to the above quote, is to try and just listen, and be a vessel of comfort.

3. GIVE YOUR OWN SELF THE MOST UNDERSTANDING.

Quite possibly, the reason we don't have the time or energy to understand one another could be because we don't have a close understanding of ourselves. Do you give yourself permission to express yourself? Do you think it's okay to feel a certain way? Be kind to yourself. Your skills in understanding others can strengthen, through practice, by learning first and foremost to understand yourself.

4. CONSIDER LEARNING TO UNDERSTAND OTHERS AS A STRENGTH, NOT AS A WEAKNESS.

Some might consider showing understanding or empathy a weakness. Question this. Think about how many quality friendships you might gain, or lives you might uplift, by becoming more understanding. As I have written before, quality relationships are shown in very recent research to be the number-one predictor of health and happiness long into old age.[101] This is one convincing reason to have more understanding in our lives.

5. REMEMBER, YOU GET BACK WHAT YOU ASK FOR.

Oprah Winfrey once wisely said, "You get in life what you have the courage to ask for." The fact of the matter is, our journeys take effort. You might be searching to be understood, or want to be more understanding towards a loved one. Whatever it is, be courageous enough to look for it, and the return might be closer than you think.

While we are each a work in progress, becoming more understanding will certainly give us more comfort and support in our lives, while strengthening close bonds. Try these five tips, and hopefully you will see the added benefit!

(*The Huffington Post*, July 2017)

4 REASONS YOU SHOULD CELEBRATE OTHERS' SUCCESS

Remember when somebody you knew received a promotion, achieved something great, or got a better job? Do you remember what you felt in that moment? Happiness? Jealousy? Now recall your last achievement or accomplishment. How good did you feel about yourself?

When the job market is competitive, or you feel like your income falls short, there are times when you might think to yourself, "Why don't I have the same status, money, or success as that person?"

But think for a minute how good it would feel if you were just as happy for another's success as your own. Why? The benefits of celebrating others' success can include creating optimism instead of feeling put down[102]—the vital protective ingredient in a recent Harvard University study.[103] Published in the *American Journal of Epidemiology*, the study looked at 70,000 women and found that a sense of optimism might reduce the risk from dying of major causes, including cardiovascular disease.

What does it mean to be just as happy for the success of others as for our own? Well, it's a matter of attitude.[104] Adopting a praising and loving attitude will help you bask in the success of those you know and with whom you feel a personal connection. This might be difficult at times, but it's a great way to help us lead more positive lives and get more in return. Learn the benefits and see how your attitude shift can boost your well-being.

1. HEALTH

If we celebrated others' success as if it were our own, we could feel a huge surge in positivity and joy, which can lead to greater optimism, the latter benefiting our own health.[105] In the previously mentioned Harvard study, an optimistic view on life was shown to protect not only against cardiovascular disease, but also prevent premature death from other major causes, such as cancer, stroke, respiratory disease, and infection.[106] Such rewards in terms of health are compelling, and they confirm there is power in positive thinking. In fact, another earlier study found that positive psychology "assets," such as optimism and positive emotions, are predictors of good physical health.[107]

2. SATISFACTION

By being courageous and selfless enough to embrace others' success, we also get the benefit of greater satisfaction.[108] We feel fulfilled instead of bitter. For example, your best friend gets a job offer at a great company and you don't know how to feel. You might feel happy, but conflicted, especially if you feel less successful at the moment. But having the courage to celebrate your friend's success as your own can lead to personal satisfaction[109] when you think, "Okay,

I now know someone who works at X company!" Your inner circle of affiliations and acquaintances grows, and you can feel appropriately satisfied by that.

According to Tai Goodwin, author of *Girlfriend, It's Your Time!: Reclaim Your Brilliance and Step Into Your Purpose*, celebrating others can improve your relationships with them as well. "Healthy relationships involve sharing both ups and downs," Goodwin writes in her *Huffington Post* article. "People are more likely to respond positively to you if they sense that you're truly happy for them."[110]

3. SUCCESS

Not only does your inner circle of affiliations grow with others' success, but you can also potentially find personal success.[111] For example, say your best friend's company is advertising for other positions. Now you have an internal referral that might benefit your own career should you desire working with the same company.[112] What's the psychology at play here?

- **We can be *mindful* of opportunities that come with others' success.** This requires an attitude and perspective adjustment.[113] You might miss out on opportunities and lose your time being bitter without changing underlying feelings and, effectively, the view you hold.
- **Conceptualizing your own success after another's success means *being sensitive* to the changes in circumstances as well.** For example, you might need to wait several months before applying for a job with Company X where your best friend was hired in order to use him or her as a referral.

4. WILLPOWER

Beyond seizing an available opportunity where possible, our sense of embracing others' achievements helps to expand our own willpower.[114] American football player and coach Vince Lombardi said, "The difference between a successful person and others is not a lack of strength, nor a lack of knowledge, but a lack of will."[115] Our own willpower, i.e. motivation, can be awakened in turn when we see the success of others.

Now, with an understanding of some of the benefits that come with celebrating others' success as your own, use these tips to put them into action.

- Write down three ways that the other person's success can be beneficial to you.
- Congratulate the other person for their success through a greeting card, social media post, gift, etc.
- Share the good news with your own family and revel in the atmosphere of positivity.

Get motivated to find your own passion and work toward greater personal success.

(*Success Magazine*, April 2017)

WHAT TO DO IF YOU OR SOMEONE YOU KNOW IS HURTING OR GRIEVING DURING THE HOLIDAYS

Do you feel like you are hurting this holiday season? Experiencing grief? Or is it someone you care about that is feeling this way? There are multiple reasons why sadness and grief might strike us this time of year. Perhaps you are experiencing the loss or absence of a loved one, being far from home, losing a job, feeling depressed, or not having enough food to put on the table.

It might seem really difficult to enjoy the season as you once did, in the middle of your pain, sadness, and grief. Here are some ways to cheer yourself up or help someone you know.

1. EXPRESS YOUR PAIN TO SOMEONE WHO LOVES AND CARES.

When we experience hurt, our current pain may feel stronger than we want it to. It's okay. One of the first steps to healing is to express your pain to someone who loves and cares for you. Burying the feeling won't help; it might resurface in unwelcome ways. Cry if you need to. It's okay. Communicate how you feel, as difficult as it might be. Your ability to confide in someone other than yourself can help dissipate the pain or move you closer to letting the pain go.

2. LOOK THROUGH OLD PHOTOS OF GOOD MEMORIES.

Maybe you have two or three such photos. However many, try to look through old photos of good memories and remind yourself: *This is temporary. Good times will eventually be here.* Whether from your kindergarten graduation, a childhood birthday, or an earlier holiday when you weren't grieving, being able to look through old photos is a great way to rekindle positive emotions. Doing so also puts into perspective the idea that times *do change*. We just have to be patient and wait out the storm.

3. REMIND YOURSELF WHAT YOU ARE GRATEFUL FOR.

Oftentimes when we are hurting, nothing feels worse. But the fact is, very often things could be much worse. Reminding ourselves of things to be grateful for is a great way to lessen hurt and grief. For example, recalling we have friends, acquaintances, or loved ones still in our life is a truly wonderful start. We can be grateful that we can walk, sleep, eat, and think. Try writing these down daily and remind yourself at the end of the week of all of what you are grateful for.

4. DO SOMETHING YOU LIKE (OR USED TO LIKE) TO CHEER YOUR MOOD.

It's as simple as that. Do something you like, or that you used to like, whether it be small or big, and see how it affects you. For example, build a card house from a pile of playing cards; or turn on your car radio and listen to some of your favorite music. If your pain is great, it might take doing this activity with a friend or loved one who cares about you to change your mood. Try. By trying, you'll have at least begun accepting your sadness or grief in order to hopefully move on. This is a great start. Be proud of yourself.

5. SEEK PROFESSIONAL HELP FOR GRIEF OR SADNESS THAT IS CONSISTENTLY THERE.

If you or someone you know is experiencing longer than expected grief or sadness and it interferes with their daily routine, try seeking professional help. This is a way to shift gears and help move forward when grief or difficulty becomes too large to bear.

We all experience pain, hurt, sadness, and grief. What we do with these emotions—accepting them, moving on, and trying again—is the most we can ask from ourselves or someone we know. Let us gain strength from our grief and sadness in this way and continue to move forward stronger.

(*GratCircle.com*, December 2019)

PART VI

HEALING

TIPS TO ELEVATE YOU WHEN YOU FEEL THE BLUES

For those of you who have felt down recently—whether about your job, yourself, or your circumstances in life in general—remember: there is always hope for a brighter and happier future. We can't always explain why a sudden challenge may force us into difficulty, whether emotionally or physically; however, there are steps you can take to feel better both in the short and long term. Try these tips.

1. EXERCISE

The natural high that we get from exercise makes us feel stronger mentally and physically. It's that simple. When we feel stronger, life looks more doable and we often lose the temporary feeling of frustration or difficulty. You feel in the moment when you task your body with a physical challenge. You focus on the present, forget about the past, and stop worrying about the future. It becomes easier to feel happy about ourselves through exercise achievements, especially when we exercise regularly and nourish workouts with a diet high in fruits, vegetables, and protein. Try working out with a group of friends or at least one friend, and the time should go by quicker than when alone. Listening to music can help pass the time if you happen to be alone.

2. NON-JUDGMENTAL MEDITATION

In order to understand our thoughts and feelings, sometimes we need introspection. Take two to eight minutes each day and let yourself clear your mind by sitting relaxed in a naturally lit space. Close your eyes and let your thoughts come naturally. Don't judge them. Then picture each thought as a cloud floating away from your mind. Repeat the thought or "cloud floating" exercise until you find a balance and begin to understand and untangle your thoughts and feelings better than before. This short meditation exercise is based on an article written by psychotherapist Jennifer Rollin.[116]

3. PICK UP HOBBIES AND PRACTICE THEM REGULARLY.

Hobbies are important because they add routine to your lifestyle and can improve self-image. If you are more athletic, try hobbies such as swimming, running, weight-lifting, biking, yoga, tennis, or hiking. If you are less athletic, try hobbies such as cooking, baking, painting, drawing, writing, playing an instrument, singing, walking outdoors, or any other relaxing hobby you might enjoy. Continue to do the hobby as regularly as twice each week. Soon, with regular upkeep, you will begin to feel like you are on the path towards achievement and self-improvement. This will help you feel better about yourself, either physically, mentally, or both. If you skip a day in the routine, don't beat yourself up about it. Try to pick up where you left off and continue to enjoy. You can show off your achievements or skills once they are improved to family or friends.

4. PRACTICE GRATITUDE STATEMENTS

When you might feel like life looks bleak and less rewarding than before, it is okay to feel down. It might take longer than you'd imagined to get back to "the way things were." Remember, however, in the peaks and valleys of life that gratitude ought to be the number one constant.

Try writing down statements of gratitude. You can write down compliments that you receive, a good deed that you did (or someone else did for you), or an achievement that you feel especially grateful for in your current circumstance. Write down three things you are grateful for in a journal or helpful app each day and read over the statements each week to boost your positivity about life and about yourself. Remember, there are always small (or big) things to be grateful for in life, no matter how difficult a situation you might be facing.

5. PERSEVERE WHILE IN DIFFICULTY

There is no substitute for perseverance when it comes to moving beyond difficulty. Day-in and day-out, there may be no explanation often for suffering or feeling down (especially when it feels like it is extremely prolonged), but remember that by moving forward you will feel ease eventually. Whether your immediate goal is to feel stronger, more confident, or overall happier, if you are persevering, you are automatically beating difficulty and showing your innermost courage. Depression and grief (or the temporary blues) do not always let go immediately; however, perseverance will ultimately help you become the strongest version of yourself.

6. CONSIDER PROFESSIONAL HELP.

If you are left with little social support or are facing an extremely difficult circumstance, you may choose to seek professional help. Consider this option if you find that a good balance of other coping strategies does not help to maintain your current lifestyle. Whether simply talking to a therapist or consulting with a medical professional, there are alternatives that can improve your emotional and mental state. Do not be scared to seek help. Remember that coping strategies (like those listed here) and social support will still ultimately carry the largest impact on your well-being.

7. FIND SOLID RELATIONSHIPS THAT WILL ALLOW YOU TO EXPRESS YOURSELF.

When we may face challenges, either small or large, we need an outlet to help us cope with our thoughts and feelings. If you have a solid social support system—through close friends, with parents, or with other family members—this will help you tremendously. Express your feelings (however difficult they may be) to trusted individuals, and let this be a source of coping. Self-expression is especially helpful when we do not feel judged by those who we trust with our personal feelings. Find good, loving, trusted individuals who will help you move forward in your struggle. Love yourself, respect yourself, and remember that when you love yourself the most, others will do the same. Keep persevering, and do not give up, no matter how difficult things get.

(*The Huffington Post*, October 2016)

COPING WITH DIFFICULTY SO THAT YOU HEAL AND STAY HEALTHY

In times of difficulty—whether it be an illness facing a loved one, a personal challenge to your health, or just a great deal of stress that you might face—there is much to be said for healthy coping mechanisms. How can we learn to cope so that we heal, in the short and long term, and stay healthy? Below are seven coping tips.

1. BE AWARE OF THE SIGNALS YOUR BODY IS GIVING YOU.

When you are facing stress, your body will tell you. You might have difficulty sleeping, get headaches, come down with an illness, or even have a fainting episode or palpitations. Take these as a sign that you need to rest and take care of yourself. If you feel like you can't take a break and reboot, remind yourself that in order to help others, you must take care of your own health. You might be able to take a five-minute break at work or encourage yourself to let go of negative habits.

2. REMEMBER THAT FACING DIFFICULTY WILL MAKE YOU A STRONGER PERSON.

Certainly, when facing stress, we all cope differently. For the greater part, if we collect ourselves to cope mostly in healthy ways—if we persevere, and find meaning in our difficulty—then we become stronger individuals. At times, suffering or stress may seem meaningless, and we might feel overwhelmed. This is a signal that we must express our emotions to get to the bottom of our struggle. While not all difficulties may feel like they build us up, the truth is that they really do, even if we can't figure that out for ourselves in the present moment. Suffering is temporary if you look at it that way (which at times may seem very difficult), but additional strength and courage last forever.

Importantly, when we cope in a healthy way, our brains become wired or rewired to be less afraid of difficulty. Our courage and strength build our character and resolve. We can help others who might be facing a challenge. We can become beacons of hope.

3. LEARN TO SAY "NO" WHEN YOU MEAN IT.

This is similar to watching the signals from your body. It is worth mentioning on its own, however. When we are coping with an illness, or helping to care for a loved one, we must not take on everything ourselves. Try to avoid pushing through when you feel completely overwhelmed or exhausted. Learn to say "no" when you mean it. You can always ask for help from a friend or neighbor.

4. FIND WAYS TO BUILD YOUR BODY EMOTIONALLY AND PHYSICALLY WHILE FACING YOUR DIFFICULTY.

Physically

First, you can exercise. This creates a natural high which supports good brain function. Second, eat plenty of colorful fruits and vegetables and nourish your body with water and other healthy fluids. Avoid too much sugar. This will help prevent your weight from fluctuating too much. See what feels right for your body. If you need to, take a warm shower or a bath to relieve some of the immediate tension.

Emotionally

Both diet and exercise can influence your resilience, and in turn, strengthen you emotionally. Other practices to help you resolve tough emotions include positive and realistic self-talk; expressing your feelings when appropriate (see tip #7); and non-judgmental meditation. For more on non-judgmental meditation, see the article entitled *Tips to Elevate You When You Feel the Blues.*

5. REMEMBER, EVERYTHING IS NOT IN YOUR CONTROL.

For many, prayer can help in times of difficulty. By praying, we remind ourselves that we are not in complete control of the circumstances; in effect, stress can be lifted from our shoulders. However, it is also important to remember that all our hopes and desires may not be fulfilled at a given time. The way our prayers are answered may be different than what we expect or want. We can renew our hope and still pray, however, by finding meaning in the response of our prayers as life continues.

6. BE IN THE PRESENT. FOCUS ON THE PRESENT. DO NOT WORRY ABOUT THE PAST OR THE FUTURE.

This is difficult for most. However, it cannot be underestimated or underemphasized. Our focus on the present alleviates worry and tension, and brings the right amount of alertness and attention to a difficulty, whatever it may be. We often lose sight of the present and grieve or worry about the past or future, but what good does this do? If needed, express your thoughts or concerns about the past or future to a loved one to let them out of your system. You can also use positive self-talk to keep you rooted in the present. For example, you might say to yourself, "I am going to enjoy this day." This is a healthy coping mechanism and helps you keep focused one day or hour at a time.

7. SELF-EXPRESSION WILL HELP YOU ALLEVIATE TENSION AND WORRY.

When we're younger, it may seem like in order to be an adult, you have to keep everything to yourself and just let your body somehow cope with it internally. When we grow older, perhaps we forget to express our emotions, given this false perspective of adulthood. It is critical to express yourself in order to avoid burnout or overwhelming emotions. Find a solid relationship in which you can express yourself completely without worry of being judged or judging yourself. Letting yourself feel emotions is vital, as is sharing with other loved ones at appropriate times.

In sum, coping mechanisms are critical, can be learned, and are needed, especially in the midst of difficulty. We can heal more quickly and stay healthy by reminding ourselves of these tips. Use proper self-care and refresh, so that you can stay a strong spirit. Surely, you will gain courage and strength that will last long into your life.

(*The Huffington Post*, November 2016)

5 REASONS TO STAY HOPEFUL, NO MATTER WHAT

Are you looking to stay hopeful, no matter what?
If you're feeling unsure of what the future will bring—whether personally, professionally, financially, emotionally, or otherwise—there may be reasons you doubt your ability to carry hope. Here's how you can challenge those feelings of doubt and give yourself reason to stay hopeful.

1. YOU HAVE UNTAPPED POTENTIAL.

When times might feel turbulent, remember to look inside. Your ability to change yourself for the better or help others might just be what you've always wanted, but didn't channel well enough. Look into your character and skill sets, and figure out how you can lift yourself first. Then, move on to lifting others, while continuing to lift yourself. Regardless of the direction you take, once you find it, your untapped potential is waiting to be discovered.

2. IF YOU CARE ENOUGH, YOU WILL SUCCEED.

For those seeking to accomplish new things and reach new heights, remember how much you care. If you care enough, some form of success or opportunity will come your way. Finding the quickest route to success might not always happen, but eventually, if you care enough, your internal GPS will reach you to your desired destination.

3. TRY TO STAY POSITIVE. POSITIVITY CAN OPEN DOORS TO SUCCESS.

If positivity doesn't come naturally to you, it is okay, you can still learn. Read up on ways to be grateful, for example, or how to strengthen your relationships. Feelings of gratitude, or staying supportive to others close to you, require a commitment to positivity you might not have known you had. This positivity eventually spreads within and around you, and personal or professional success can often follow.

4. DREAM BIG, BUT TAKE SMALL, VALUABLE STEPS TOWARD ACTUALIZING YOUR GOALS.

A large part of staying hopeful is dreaming big. You may have goals for yourself, or how to help others, or both. The part that most people forget is to take small, valuable steps as often as possible towards making those goals come to life. Remember, it can help to bounce your thoughts off an inner circle of friends and family as needed to readjust your efforts. Keep dreaming, readjusting, and stay focused to reach your goals. You can do it.

5. REMEMBER, THERE ARE MANY OPPORTUNITIES TO SEIZE.

Whether you strive to become a chef, an athlete, a musician, a writer, or a physician, the opportunities abound. You might want to earn a certification, seize a new job, finish high school, or expand your social networks. Whatever path you're on, keep searching for your sweet spot, and harness that strength once you find it in order to seize as many opportunities as you can.

Hopefully, the five above reasons will give you a good dose of two traits: positivity and drive. Staying hopeful is a matter of maintaining both. While it may be difficult at times, you will go far with your efforts.

(*The Huffington Post*, December 2017)

6 WAYS TO BETTER UNDERSTAND (AND ALSO CARE FOR) YOURSELF

Do you feel like life can be too rough? Do you feel like you could deal with tough circumstances in a better way? How often do you encourage yourself to push through difficult or stressful times? Maybe you could use a better understanding of self—or self-awareness—to create more motivation.

Here are six ways to better understand—and also care for—yourself, and, in turn, make it through the stress and challenges that come your way.

1. IDENTIFY WHAT IS YOUR BIGGEST STRESSOR, AND ACCEPT IT.

If you are going through a tough and uncertain period in your life, try to identify what it is that creates feelings of doubt, stress, frustration, etc. Once you feel like you've got a good grasp, tell yourself that you *accept it.* Repeat the thought process daily and this could help you feel more productive and positive.

2. LET GO OF YOUR CONCERNS DURING DOWN TIME.

If you have a lot on your mind, and work seems to frustrate, remember that your concerns don't need to eat up your down time. When going to sleep, or on weekends (if you're not working), you will be far better off letting go of your worries. How so? Consider encouraging self-talk reminding yourself to "let it go," or chose to focus on at least one thing you are grateful for at night. Also, make sure to spend down-time enjoying yourself with those you care about, and who care about you. Recharging is essential.

3. CONFIDE IN YOUR CLOSEST FRIENDS AND FAMILY WHO CARE FOR YOU.

It is crucial to express our emotions to loved ones if, when, and before we get overwhelmed. Make sure to take time to express yourself. Self-expression can help you identify bottled-up emotions. This is also crucial for recharging. If finding the right person is difficult, consider a health professional.

4. REMEMBER, SUCCESS IS IN MAINTAINING PERSONAL GROWTH DURING THE JOURNEY AND NOT ONLY ACHIEVED BY REACHING YOUR END GOAL.

It is easy to feel like success is defined by reaching an endpoint or destination. By thinking this way, we can lose focus of how rewarding the journey can be for us. Money, fame, status, and education are easy to be consumed by. However, the growth process while being guided on your journey can afford the greatest satisfaction day-in and day-out. Keep your eyes on personal growth, and the rewards will feel even richer when you make it to the finish line.

5. REMEMBER, PUTTING IN THE EFFORT IS IN YOUR CONTROL.

Whether you are becoming more self-aware, writing down goals, or committing time to office meetings, putting in effort and taking a shot at bigger goals—like a promotion, new house, or new business—is the most you could ask from yourself. Perhaps some times you will have a little more luck compared to other instances. You are really doing the best you can do by putting in the effort. Remind yourself of that.

6. STAY GROUNDED IN WHO YOU ARE IN ORDER TO STAY SELF-AWARE.

When change affects us, we may each react differently. The best thing to do is stay grounded in who you are in order to feel the most self-aware. Rather than being controlled by outside factors such as fame, status, or money, your understanding of self will help you prevail during transitions and be truly successful.

These are six ways for those seeking to better understand and care for themselves. Hopefully, if applied, these tips can bring added focus, satisfaction, and benefit!

(*The Huffington Post*, October 2017)

5 TIPS TO ENJOY THE PRESENT MOMENT

Do you find yourself concerned too often about the past or future? How often are you able to let go and absorb yourself in the present moment? While distant issues weigh us down from time to time, wouldn't it be satisfying to learn how to simply live in, and hopefully enjoy, the present moment? If you're having trouble, here are five ways that can help.

1. ADOPT A CAREFREE ATTITUDE

While all social engagements don't allow us to let loose entirely, wouldn't it be nice if we gave ourselves permission to kick back with a less controlling attitude? Adopting a carefree attitude on a night out with a spouse, or during a family vacation, for example, could allow you to free yourself from stress or preoccupation, and capitalize on your enjoyment. Try it out, and perhaps it could save you from some needless fret.

2. REVERSE YOUR ROLES

When you feel like it might be hard to be in the present moment, think for a second about reversing your roles. "What would I want them to say to me?" you might wonder during a conversation when you find your mind distracted. Then return to the present conversation by displaying respect and empathy for the other person. Not only will this help build your communication and understanding skills in the process, but you stay in the moment *and* the empathy and respect you use can build a meaningful connection.

3. ENGAGE IN DELICIOUSLY POSITIVE SELF-TALK.

Engaging in positive self-talk can keep your spirits higher than average, especially in the present moment. For example, tell yourself: "This is okay. I am doing well," if you're feeling nervous. Alternatively, you might say: "Things could be much worse. I am grateful for this moment." Thinking in terms of gratitude is one of the best ways to bring yourself to the present moment. Why not try it? Positive self-talk can prime the pathways in your brain to experience positive emotions—such as gratitude—more often.

4. ACKNOWLEDGE ALL THE DIFFERENT EMOTIONS IN YOURSELF AND IN OTHERS.

As humans, we each feel a wide array of emotions. When we acknowledge emotions in ourselves and verbally or nonverbally in others, we demonstrate that we see value in and understand ourselves and others. Try to acknowledge feelings, listen, and be there for yourself first; and then, for others. Showing acknowledgment in this way can be very liberating, releasing baggage from your shoulders and allowing meaningful connections to take place with so many others. And again, it will help you to experience the rich benefits of staying present.

5. STRIVE TO LEAD A HEALTHY LIFESTYLE

In order to get the most from the present, our physical and mental selves need to be nourished and treated well. Part of this comes from leading a healthy lifestyle by eating and sleeping well, and, hopefully, exercising. Another part comes with being a part of social engagements and maintaining positive social circles. Try to maintain these, and you'll get even more from the present moment.

Certainly, this is not an exhaustive list for how to enjoy the present moment, but it is a worthwhile start. Curious to see if these ways help you? The return on investment is well worth the effort.

(*GratCircle.com*, January 2018)

4 WAYS TO MOVE PAST HURT AND REJECTION

Have you ever dealt with hurt or rejection? If you're like most people, you likely have. Moving ahead, however, can be challenging. Having the right mindset or grit can help, along with other tools.

Bestselling self-help author Karen Salmansohn says, "Often it's the deepest pain which empowers you to grow into your highest self." If you've suffered hurt, rejection, or loss, finding happiness and joy (perhaps in the state before your hurt or loss) can be a difficult journey. However long the journey may be, recovering from hurt helps us become what Salmansohn describes as our "highest self."

Here are four ways to keep moving along in your journey towards joy and success, including ways to make things easier as you do.

1. DON'T MINIMIZE YOUR FEELINGS. HONOR THEM.

When we suffer from hurt, loss, or rejection, some of us might be inclined to deny how we feel. However, denial and minimization of raw and difficult feelings keep us from moving onward. Psychology professor Steven C. Hayes of *Psychology Today* says, "Suppression and avoidance [of pain and loss] come at a high cost—they diminish our ability to do much of anything else."[117]

Honor your feelings by letting them out. You might let out tears, frustration, sympathy, anger, or a combination of all the above. It's okay.

2. LET GO OF THE PAST.

Whether sweet or bitter, past memories can keep you from enjoying the present. Letting go, as motivational speaker Tony Robbins writes, can help us reach our "true potential."[118] Let go of what was (when it interferes with your ability to enjoy the present); take that ticket, move ahead, and go for the ride, anticipating that the best is yet to come.

3. FIND YOUR PURPOSE.

Hurt and loss can help us find our purpose. Trying to find yours may take time, but once found, think how tremendously motivating it can be. As Pablo Picasso said, "The meaning of life is to find your gift. The purpose of life is to give it away."

4. LEARN FROM REJECTION AND CHALLENGE.

I see one of the wisest ways of honoring challenging feelings from hurt or rejection is by learning from them. Perhaps a kind gesture made you want to pay it forward. Perhaps your suffering helped you connect with others in a similar position.

Learning and growing lets you achieve more, and continuously doing so is a great recipe for a joyful and grateful life. Let yourself learn. Keep on growing.

In sum, these four ways to move past hurt and rejection can make your present all that much more rewarding and joyful. Empower yourself. With gratitude and with strength, you can move forward towards your "highest self."

(*GratCircle.com*, February 2020)

WHY LIFE CIRCUMSTANCES DON'T CHANGE YOU, BUT ASK YOU TO STAY TRUE TO WHO YOU ARE

Life gives and gives. It rarely takes away, if we are paying close attention. How, you ask? Well, Shakespeare wrote, "To thine own self be true." Can we give credence to his famous saying in each of our lives? Perhaps, yes, if we remember our true nature—our only "true north."

Our true nature is presented via the gift of life. As we grow, circumstances in our lives will give us the downs and ups in life that are most common, but often unspoken. It is up to us to take from life the gifts that it presents, even if they are presented as challenges.

As my beloved grandmother said often, "Take in the good, but leave out the bad." She wasn't being just precise; she was so precisely wise.

While we think we lose things in life—perhaps money; status; health of ourselves, our parents, our kids; material goods; you name it—we actually are given a test to see how much we can stay true to ourselves. That is, if we are fortunate to have discovered some of our best qualities. (See more about discovering innate qualities in *Life Foundations 101: Appreciating Personal Identity and Internal Coping Mechanisms.*) Staying true to our best qualities will keep us from *actually* losing hope, from *actually* losing health, from *actually* losing what we think it is that we thought we lost.

Perhaps a lost limb has affected your sense of identity, and your ability to move ahead. But there is not a single question. Our qualities are not defined by a limb or a body part. We are more than our individual parts. Our qualities lie in our hearts, foremost, and are conveyed by our actions and words. The true test of our lives is if we are happy with ourselves, our ability to "be true," no matter whatever loss we think we may have endured. Indeed, life gives and gives. Our only job is to learn this and remember it when circumstances feel like they hit our shores of individuality.

(*GratCircle.com*, September 2019)

8 WAYS TO ACTUALLY KEEP YOU HAPPY

The familiar saying of 'nature versus nurture' applies to keeping our happiness at the levels we want. While it is true that 50 percent of our happiness is rooted in our genetics, about the same amount of our happiness comes from our own intentional activities—that is, 40 percent.[119] *We have 40 percent control over our own happiness—more than we might think. So, what can you do to actually keep yourself happy?*

The 2011 documentary *Happy* by Academy Award-nominated producer and director Roko Belic introduced the idea that we have a say in our happiness levels. The movie was inspired by a colleague of Belic's, Tom Shadyac, who noticed that the U.S. was twenty-third on a *New York Times* list of the happiest countries, despite its massive amount of wealth.[120] It seems Shadyac was interested in exploring what actually makes and keeps people happy.

The movie *Happy* explores the science behind happiness: from neurotransmitters in our brains; to what explains differences in happiness among identical twins; to expert interviews with psychologists.

A striking take-home lesson is that only 10 percent of our happiness comes from money, health, status, or other life circumstances.

Given a 40 percent stake in determining our happiness, the question lingers: What can we do to keep ourselves happy?

Sonja Lyubomirsky is a professor of psychology at the University of California, Riverside, and the author of *The How of Happiness: A Scientific Approach to Getting the Life You Want*, a book with scientifically-backed strategies to help people increase their happiness levels. Lyubomirsky observes that happy people:

- Nurture and enjoy their social relationships
- Are comfortable expressing gratitude
- Practice optimism about the future
- Savor pleasures and live in the present moment
- Make physical activity a habit
- Are often spiritual or religious
- Are deeply committed to meaningful goals.[121]

According to Lyubomirsky, here are eight ways we can actually keep our happiness levels higher than usual.

1. EXPRESS GRATITUDE.

Realizing the good things in our lives, or counting our blessings, actually affects our happiness levels. We may express our gratitude verbally or in writing; or via a spiritual or religious habit, such as meditation or prayer. Cultivating a habit of thankfulness can be refreshing at any time, though especially when we may need the reminder, such as in times of difficulty.

2. DEVELOP OPTIMISM

Developing a sense of optimism can reward our physical and mental health more than we think. Even if we are not always rewarded immediately, the feel-good effects of optimism can leave us hopeful about the future. Similar to how in sports a coach may say, "Imagine yourself making the shot," to breed a winning mentality, optimism about the future can elicit greater mental toughness and grit so that you may reach your goals, whether they are personal or professional.

3. PRACTICE ACTS OF KINDNESS

By extending a helping hand to strangers or a loved one, an act of kindness, small or large, can be emotionally rewarding. You can practice sharing a smile more than usual; a simple smile can bring more joy than you think to someone feeling down.

4. NURTURE RELATIONSHIPS

Relationships may not come easily, but if taken care of, they can be rewarding in multiple ways. In tough times, such as illness, loved ones can reciprocate kindness by cooking a meal. Friends can remind you of your strengths and what they love about your character. Simple, meaningful conversations that come with the nurturing of relationships can satisfy and further boost your happiness levels.

5. DEVELOP STRATEGIES FOR COPING

The ability to carry yourself in tough times can involve everything from exercise to self-expression to non-judgmental meditation.

Experience often tells us what works best for us. Rather than going through necessary hardship, however, to learn our coping strategies, we can become aware of potential "go-to coping strategies" by taking note of character strengths, and how to enrich and nurture them further. For example, you might find hobbies, or work towards goals that complement and accentuate your strengths. If you are skilled at reading, you might try and read three to five books in a month. You can try and help yourself cope through hardship this way.

6. INCREASE FLOW EXPERIENCES AND BE ABSORBED IN THE PRESENT.

Lyubomirsky writes in her book, "When in flow, people report feeling strong and efficacious, at the peak of their abilities, alert, in control, and completely unselfconscious. They do the activity for the sheer sake of doing it."[122] Have you ever felt this way? Try picking up a hobby such as writing, painting, exercise, baking, or cooking—to name a few—so that you'll feel this way regularly; or, think back to when you felt this way before and expand upon those experiences.

7. COMMIT TO YOUR GOALS.

Working toward goals is a multistep process. First, laying out goals takes self-reflection and identification of ways you can reach your goal. Second, you must keep at it. Sometimes you will be rewarded, sometimes you won't. It takes stamina and hard work. Third, you might need to adjust and self-reflect again on your goals as you reevaluate what is important to you. It is a process, but working at it feels great, especially when you see that it might be helping others.

8. TAKE CARE OF YOUR MIND AND BODY

Meditation, exercise, and sleeping properly are examples of ways we can take care of our mind and body. Other ways may include eating well and self-expression. Being aware of the signals our bodies give us (e.g., difficulty sleeping, headaches, weight gain) is important so we know when to make a change. Each of us has varying priorities, so our strategies in taking care of our bodies will vary—with good reason. Do your best to keep your mind and body as healthy as possible.

All together, above are eight evidence-based ways we can keep ourselves happy. Remember that happiness may temporarily come when life circumstances change for the better, though it may not linger the way we want it to. In order to actually keep us happy, we can and should work at it through the ways listed above or other proven strategies. Remember, 40 percent of it is up to us!

(*The Huffington Post*, March 2017)

THE GLOBAL MENTAL HEALTH MOVEMENT BY CELEBRITIES AND INDIVIDUALS

Increasingly, television and social media have brought home greater awareness of the often-private challenges faced by Hollywood celebrities and average individuals alike. Advocacy of mental health has risen in recent years, but still needs greater worldwide attention, awareness, and thoughtful discussion. Mental health has been championed in recent years by royal figures including the Duke and Duchess of Cambridge, Prince Harry, and First Lady Michelle Obama. Rising attention by celebrities, professionals, and individuals means one thing: a new norm in society is needed in order to drive home greater awareness, empathy and solutions around mental health stigma and treatment. What should you know to embrace the new norm of awareness and no-stigma?

Remember the importance of these three things: awareness, empathy, and being non-judgmental to those in need of or receiving help.

1. AWARENESS

Here are some key facts to know when it comes to awareness on the subject of global mental health.

- World Mental Health Day is October 10th each year.
- Medical school departments, in particular, of psychiatry and global health at schools such as George Washington University and Harvard University offer education in global mental health.
- A 2013 New England Journal of Medicine (NEJM) article stated that the "deeply institutionalized stigma surrounding the field of mental health is being challenged and overcome," offering hope to those suffering in silence and to those able to receive help.[123]
- Depression is the third leading contributor to the global disease burden.[124]
- The United Nation's Sustainable Development Goals (SDGs) post-2015 agenda includes "promoting mental health as well as reducing mental illness." The SDGs support mental health awareness and changing the status quo, particularly via Target 3.4, which aims to "promote mental health and well-being" all the way until 2030.[125]
- Globally, there are an estimated 450 million people with a mental, neurological, or substance-use (MNS) condition according to the American Psychological Association (APA), and the majority lack quality mental health services.[126]
-

2. GAINING EMPATHY

You can join the advocacy work of celebrities such as the Duke and Duchess of Cambridge, along with Prince Harry, who have demonstrated their commitment to raising awareness around mental health simply by gaining a greater sense of empathy to those affected. In April 2016, the British Royals announced the #HeadsTogether campaign, a charity that aims to end the stigma around mental health, which was chosen as the 2017 London Marathon Charity of the Year.[127]

"Mental health is just as important as physical health," the Duchess has said in a public service announcement for the charity.

Clearly, the British Royals share in caring about mental health and are trying to do their part—a lesson to all those who seek to be more empathetic. With greater empathy for those seeking or in need of help, hopefully more individuals will seek access to quality services and be able to lead more fulfilling lives.

3. BEING NON-JUDGMENTAL

Many other celebrities in the U.S.—including Demi Lovato, Wayne Brady, and Catherine Zeta-Jones—have spoken to the issue of removing stigma. "There is no shame in receiving help," Catherine Zeta-Jones said in 2015. First Lady Michelle Obama has also been an outspoken advocate for mental health awareness. "Whether an illness affects your heart, your leg, or your brain, it's still an illness, and there should be no distinction," the First Lady stated.[128]

Last, Kate Middleton spoke to the issue of childhood mental health when she articulately stated, "A child's mental health is just as important as their physical health and deserves the same quality of support. No one would feel embarrassed about seeking help for a child if they broke their arm."[129] With the wave in advocacy by US celebrities, political figures, and royalty alike, hopefully those in need are more likely to seek help, while others can do their part by staying non-judgmental.

Ultimately, with the three qualities of awareness, empathy, and being non-judgmental affixed to your sleeve, you'll be ready more than ever to help celebrities, professionals, and individuals alike spread the new norm of stigma-free awareness. Join and help spread the awareness, empathy, and non-judgmental mindset!

(*The Huffington Post*, August 2016)

PART VII

“ALL GOOD THINGS”

10 WAYS TO BE MORE KIND

Do you find it challenging to be kind? Maybe in certain circumstances compared to others? When we express authentic kindness to a friend, coworker or even stranger, we project that version of ourselves that others will likely remember. Think about how it felt the last time you received a kind gesture. Then, think about how amazing it would be if the feeling was spread the world over.

Here are ten ways to be more kind.

1. WHEN YOU BELIEVE IN SOMEONE, TELL THEM DIRECTLY. CONVEY YOUR SUPPORT TO THEM.

Let's say we all supported and believed in the ability of our friends and family to do amazing things. Put another way, think about how your support could drive even one person to achieve things greater than themselves. Imagine how much the world could benefit—quite simply, a lot more.

2. CONSIDER KINDNESS BEFORE YOU SPEAK.

When we may have something in our minds to say about someone and it isn't kind, remember to choose kindness before speaking. It is not a sign of weakness to choose kindness. It is a sign of heart.

3. SPREAD KINDNESS THAT YOU HAVE RECEIVED.

When we receive kindness, we may feel special about ourselves. If you can, in some way or another, continue to spread the kindness that you have received, it is a great way to pay it forward.

4. BE MINDFUL OF HOW YOU TREAT OTHERS.

Considering our closest relationships, as well as our relationships with acquaintances and others who we don't see regularly, it is important to be mindful of how we treat others because of the impact it can have. Truly being considerate can go a long way with many friendships and relationships.

5. DON'T DISCRIMINATE WHO TO BE KIND TO.

As we all know, each of us is facing a challenge, whether seen or unseen. Don't discriminate who to be kind to, despite differences.

6. SET AN EXAMPLE.

What better of a role model to someone else than someone who is frankly, always kind? Try to set an example. Without role models who are kind, there would be less kindness to spread around.

7. PRACTICE GOOD INTENTIONS.

When you say something nice to someone else, remember your intention counts as well. Try to carry good intentions with displays of kindness. Kindness and good intention usually come hand in hand, but in the few cases where they could not be aligned, try to practice good intentions, like not expecting anything in return for your gesture or compliment.

8. FEEL GOOD ABOUT IT.

If you have a tougher time showing kindness, try and remember to feel good about showing this side of you. When you feel good, the act will come more regularly and spread more positivity within you.

9. REACH OUT WHEN IT IS LESS LIKELY OTHERS WILL.

If you feel like an act of kindness might be going against the grain, try to be the first to show the niceness. It will likely be as rewarding in return.

10. TRY TO BE KIND EVERY DAY.

When in doubt, be kind as often as possible, hopefully every day so that you can reap the rewards in terms of your quality of relationships and just pure satisfaction that you have spread joy to another person's life.

In all, try these ten ways to be more kind. No doubt you might still have difficulties or challenges that come your way, but with the joy of spreading kindness, your mind and heart can benefit and you can feel satisfied more often. Enjoy!

(*The Huffington Post*, November 2017)

4 TIPS ON HOW TO MAINTAIN HUMILITY WHILE STAYING CONFIDENT

In short, humility is the acceptance, acknowledgment, and understanding of our shortcomings as individuals and differences with others. As essential as it is to learn and exude confidence in our character, humility is even more important to maintain while staying confident.

Often, why we need humility is understood through experience. For example, if we experience a setback that is a blow to our ego, moving forward we might have less of an ego and a degree of humbleness in our perspective in life. Ultimately, the push and pull between and humility and confidence comes with the waxing and waning of life's trials and tribulations; enough awareness of this can lead to wisdom.

Becoming familiar with humility can help us keep a fresher and more realistic outlook on our journey in the world. Importantly, the best blend of humility and confidence can encourage us to dream and do wonderful things, all while staying humble and levelheaded.

What are some key ways to maintaining humility? Below are

four tips to consider.

1. UNDERSTAND THAT WE HAVE SHORTCOMINGS AS INDIVIDUALS.

When we reflect on ourselves, we have so much to take in. From our daily mix of emotions, to worrying about our responsibilities, to considering how well our relationships are doing, there is just so much to take in. Do we like who we are? Perhaps that question comes up every time we look in the mirror. The best way to retain humility is to recall that we could not have been taught everything as kids. Circumstances in life arise; journeys get difficult temporarily and test us—but we do not have all the answers. Our shortcomings may be that we are too tough on ourselves, do not take care of ourselves, or do not consider others' feelings, perhaps. There could be a combination of shortcomings. Regardless, the realization that we have shortcomings and accepting there are perhaps plenty is an essential first step to gaining humility.

2. BE OKAY WITH THE NOTION THAT OUR IMPERFECTIONS MAKE US HUMAN.

Beyond identifying and accepting our shortcomings, another critical step in retaining humility is to rationalize that these imperfections make us human. Our acceptance that being imperfect is okay and natural is significant. It gives us room to ask for help. *We can grow.* We can work on our imperfections to reveal bolder, stronger, and tougher versions of ourselves to the world.

3. REMEMBER THAT WE ARE NO MORE OR NO LESS THAN OTHERS WHO WE KNOW, AND WE ARE UNIQUE IN OUR OWN WAYS.

Sure, everyone has a unique character and may present themselves a certain way. There are hundreds of different people we interact with in our lives. How can we assume to know what they are handling? Or how they were raised? Or what their background is? When we interact with others, it is worth remembering these differences aren't apparent on the surface. We can give pause before making quick judgments about their character. It is a sign of humility to treat others with respect and understanding, acknowledging these differences and putting them aside for the common good.

4. REMIND OURSELVES THAT WE ARE ON A UNIQUE JOURNEY TO OUR DESTINIES.

There is constant bombardment about what success looks like in terms of wealth, career achievements, lifestyle, and more. The best thing to remind ourselves, despite whatever setbacks, is to love and build our own character along this unique journey, while maintaining humility and possibly touching others' lives in the most uplifting and positive of ways. It is worth reminding ourselves that success cannot be measured in terms of achievement unless it is guided by a good character.

The next time you experience a setback, remember that regaining confidence is just as important as acquiring humility. You may have shortcomings—imperfections that make you human; but acknowledge you are no more or less than others around you, and understand you are on a unique journey to your destiny. Keep these tips in mind, and hopefully you will be ready to take on new opportunities and embrace life's adventures.

(*The Huffington Post*, November 2016)

5 TIPS TO ENJOY EXERCISE

Do you work out? How often do you look forward to time spent exercising? Could you use some motivation to have more frequent and enjoyable workouts?

Most of us entertain the thought of working out and getting in shape; but few of us actually initiate exercise, and perhaps fewer enjoy their time working out. Here are five tips to help you enjoy exercising.

1. ASK A FRIEND OR FAMILY MEMBER TO WORK OUT WITH YOU.

Asking a friend or family member to join you in your workout can help keep you accountable, or can simply be good company. Think about it the next time you are considering skipping out on the gym.

2. EAT LITTLE DIRECTLY BEFORE YOUR WORKOUTS—PERHAPS SOME FRUIT OR CEREAL; ENJOY LOOKING FORWARD TO A HEALTHY, SATIATING MEAL AFTERWARDS, ESPECIALLY AFTER INTENSE WORKOUTS.

Nourishment with a good source of protein and fueling carbohydrates can help build muscle and give you long-lasting energy, respectively. Enjoy your food, but try to avoid large pre-exercise meals; rather, enjoy a post-exercise meal with a balanced portion from all food groups. Stay hydrated with water throughout the day, and consider a sports drink or protein shake for extra energy (if you can) while working out.

3. REMEMBER TO INCLUDE STRETCHING BEFORE (AND POSSIBLY AFTER) YOUR WORKOUTS. THIS INCLUDES BOTH STATIC AND DYNAMIC STRETCHING IN ORDER TO GET YOUR BODY'S OXYGEN FLOWING.

Stretching helps release endorphins, or "happy chemicals," and can help alleviate possible feelings of stress and depression. It is recommended to use dynamic stretching, or stretching with quick, rapid movements, to warm up the body before a workout; and static stretching, or stretching with longer, held poses, after a workout to help promote relaxation of muscles.[130]

Use care if you are not as flexible, but sustain stretching to help promote a "feel-good" feeling that will keep you coming back to the gym.

4. PUSH YOURSELF DURING A WORKOUT WHEN YOU ARE FEELING GOOD ENOUGH, BUT WITHOUT FEELING PAIN. IF RUNNING, ADD IN WALK BREAKS. YOU WILL FEEL ENDORPHINS COLLECT DURING WALK BREAKS, OR AFTER A WORKOUT, THAT WILL GENERATE A POSITIVE, RELAXING MEMORY OF YOUR WORKOUT AND LEAVE YOU CRAVING MORE.

Importantly, each person has to work within their own limits when it comes to working out. Having a good workout means pushing yourself when you are feeling strong and capable. If you feel pain, or have other hesitations, this might not apply to you. However, regular exercise and occasional intense exercise can keep you craving the gym again, largely because of the positive, strengthening, and relaxing feelings that are generated after the workout.

5. EASE INTO INITIAL WORKOUTS WHEN STARTING UP AFTER A LONG REST PERIOD. IF YOU'VE BEEN A REGULAR AT THE GYM, SET UP INCREASINGLY MORE CHALLENGING GOALS SO YOU FEEL LIKE YOU'RE ACHIEVING MORE.

If you find yourself skipping a row of exercise days, you may need to ease back into a regular routine. If you are a regular gym-goer, then consider a fun activity such as an organized run, a recreational sport, or lessons to keep you socially entertained and active. For example, a 10K with a friend or swimming lessons might be enjoyable.

Whether you're new to working out, or a fitness guru, try to build in exercise and a tasty and nutritious diet so you're excited by the idea of being healthy. Hopefully, these five tips can keep you on track to meet your fitness goals!

(*The Huffington Post*, September 2017)

5 QUESTIONS YOU MAY ASK YOURSELF BEFORE GIVING BACK

If you're looking for a way to make an impact on others, whether through your career, in your spare time, or both, perhaps start with this broad question: what are your own experiences and motivation? Considering the notion that we are each uniquely suited to make an impact, try to give yourself some time to think about what makes you feel satisfied doing, doing repeatedly, and with motivation that comes relatively easily. Then ask yourself these five questions if you want to give back.

1. WHAT EXPERIENCES DO YOU HAVE THAT HAVE SHAPED YOUR CONFIDENCE?

This can be academically-speaking, professionally-speaking, based on personal experience, hobby-based, or a mix of more than one of these. If you can figure out what has really hit your core in terms of experiences, this will help tremendously in figuring out what really makes you uniquely suited to give back. For example, if you are an accomplished marathon runner, you have the special talent of knowing how to take care of your body to hopefully prevent injury;

eating right to fuel your energy; and building the self-discipline to run regularly, among other things. Eventually, you might consider training others to run marathons or giving advice, even if not necessarily as a full-fledged career. You can give back in some way, shape, or form as part of your weekly or monthly routine. This will help you feel greatly satisfied, and you may even consider turning it into a career, if it becomes that strong of a passion.

2. ARE YOU ABLE TO TURN YOUR MOTIVATION OR EXPERIENCES INTO A SERVICE (MONEY-MAKING OR NOT)?

This comes into play when you consider the actual way of giving back. You may have a wealth of knowledge and experience, which makes you quite capable, but how are you willing to transfer your knowledge and experience to others? Would it be through creating an illustrated children's book, or through writing a memoir? How else? Here you might consider your skill sets, which I have written about in a separate article. (See *3 Steps to Figure Out Your Ideal Career*.) Skill sets, which you ought to have successfully demonstrated to yourself through projects, internships, or other experience, will clue you in on what exact service you might want to provide. For example, you might use writing, drawing, performing, or baking as part of the treasure chest of skills you can put to use in your service to others. The service may even take the shape of an online business or blog. Try to pinpoint your possible service by writing down your thoughts or talking to a trusted friend or loved one.

3. DO YOU HAVE THE MOTIVATION TO SUCCEED IN GIVING BACK IN YOUR UNIQUE WAY?

When you have identified a service you can provide to help others, like giving advice for new marathon runners, are you motivated to perform your service repeatedly? Answering "yes" to this question ought to be easy, but oftentimes we can struggle to meet other priorities, such as paying monthly bills and fulfilling family obligations. Considering your other obligations, do you see a path to making your service happen?

The more you are motivated, the more successful you could be. Going back and figuring out what really has shaped your talents, confidence, or other personal strengths will help you resoundingly answer this question with a big, fat "yes." Managing other priorities will hopefully come more easily with this motivation. If you want to hone your service or skills over time, motivation will also be very helpful.

4. DO YOU HAVE THE SOCIAL SUPPORT SYSTEM TO HELP YOU KEEP GIVING BACK SUCCESSFULLY?

This is a good question. The reason is because when we are isolated, usually our ability to share joy or express the difficulty of a struggle with others becomes more challenging. When we have a social support system, we can find more encouragement and feedback—essentially, the cushion in our seat behind the table of success; not necessarily monetary success, but the kind of personal success and positive reinforcement of giving back that leaves you feeling good.

5. ARE YOU READY TO FEEL SATISFIED AND REWARDED?

This is a rhetorical question—of course you are!

By asking yourself these five questions, you can truly begin your journey to give back in ways you find particularly rewarding, for yourself and for others. Hopefully, this will happen for you in due time!

(*The Huffington Post*, April 2017)

3 STEPS TO RUNNING A HALF-MARATHON

Hearing the words "one mile left" never felt so sweet. I was on the home stretch towards finishing my first half-marathon, and actually replied, *"Wow!"* The training had paid off. After hearing those words, seeing the finish line in sight, and then finally making it across, there are at least three steps I've learned that can be helpful if you want to run your first half-marathon or just become more athletic.

1. LEARN FROM RUNNING EXPERTS (OR FITNESS SITES), BOTH ONLINE AND IN PRINT.

It can be exciting to embark on training that will test you mentally and physically. However, if you want to train cautiously—preventing injury and increasing chances at successful workouts—you ought to learn and keep learning. I picked up a book by Jeff Galloway, an Olympian runner, and read through the parts that I thought were important for me. I was also convinced by *Competitor* magazine that running "several half-marathons" was a must before attempting anything further. (I had run a 10k years earlier.) My book and magazine were in print, but I also learned from popular online websites like *Runner's World* and others.

2. FIND A BALANCED DEGREE OF TRAINING—WHAT WORKS FOR YOU, ULTIMATELY.

Remember that exercise can make you feel great. The endorphins that collect after a workout are natural "feel-good" chemicals that can help improve your mood.[131] They can create feelings of happiness, provide willpower, and boost confidence.[132] If you ever feel sluggish, going to the gym is a great way to boost your attitude and "can-do" sense. At the same time, you don't want to overdo your training. Find what works for you. Running about three times a week was recommended by Jeff Galloway, so that's what I chose to do to prepare for my half-marathon.

3. WORK TOWARD PREVENTING INJURY AND STAYING HEALTHY.

You may encounter body signals, like knee, hip, or ankle discomfort during training or exercise that are important to be aware of. It may be wise to consult health experts, who can provide tips and exercises to help alleviate the discomfort and help you continue your training. They may also tell you to rest or even not run. Prepare yourself. For myself, after months of regular running and then two months of training, I was ready to run the half-marathon. It is recommended, for anyone looking to pick up long distances or more intense exercise, to listen to body aches and discomforts in order to prevent injury and stay healthy.[133] By staying healthy, you can ensure a greater number of positive workouts and hopefully wonderful memories.

So, get ready to stay in shape and enjoy working out! You can do it!

(*The Huffington Post*, May 2017)

4 WAYS TO FIND EXCITEMENT IN YOUR LIFE

The hustle and routine of daily life gets us from one stop to another, but how engaged are we in those activities? Are you looking for more excitement in your life? Try these tips to see if you can become more enthusiastic about where you'll be headed next.

1. USING SELF-DISCIPLINE

Self-discipline is a key ingredient that we bring to daily living. We may experience exciting moments less without regularly applying it. Whether it is training for a half-marathon, polishing your resume, searching for that next opportunity, or just maintaining relationships, everything from our jobs to our social lives requires self-discipline. The more we exercise discipline, the more we create opportunity. And more opportunity can be exciting. For example, going through a job hunt can take time and be exhausting, but the excitement of receiving an offer—especially in a field we are passionate about—makes it worth the effort.

Try creating more self-discipline in your life by investing in goals for yourself, such as career, relationship, or body goals.[134] You can develop a road map for where you want to be headed, including the steps you need to take. Self-discipline will follow more easily. You'll have activities that keep you busy, and meanwhile you can stay excited about actually reaching your goals.

2. OUR RELATIONSHIPS

Your relationships are helpful in taking you to the next level of joy and excitement. Maybe you got a new job and you want to share the good news with others, which can create excitement. Or perhaps it's something else. Maybe you are about to add a new member to your family and want to share your delight. Whatever it may be, wouldn't it be special to share your joy with others? The happiness and exhilaration we feel when our loved ones and friends reach milestones makes those milestones more special and worthwhile. Relationships can heighten our level of excitement if we nurture them and share our joys.

Try directing your relationships toward this unique kind of excitement if you can. If you don't have a milestone to share, you can enjoy a shared adventure with a friend, like volunteering at a local soup kitchen or walking a 5K. You will build a lifetime of wonderful memories this way.

3. BEING GRATEFUL

Being grateful can be another sweet ingredient for creating excitement. Try to remind yourself of what to be grateful for, regularly, at a convenient time, and wait for the helpful benefits to come.

For example, before going to sleep you could remind yourself to be grateful for available love, comfort, support, food, and water, if you are so lucky. There is a wealth of psychological research that ties gratitude to increased happiness,[135] as well as other positive emotions, including excitement.[136] Practicing gratitude can work that muscle in your brain to receive such positive emotions more often. It may sound tedious or demanding to practice gratitude regularly, but it is well worth the effort.

If you don't feel as happy or excited about where you are at, reflection on what you want can motivate you to pursue what will make you happier. Your achievements that follow can lead to greater appreciation and hopefully excitement.

4. THINKING AHEAD

This tip may sound somewhat too general or vague, but thinking ahead or regularly planning out the next steps in your day, week, or month can help build excitement in your life. For example, if you plan on meeting your deadlines for the day in the office and enjoying your cup of green tea at the end of the day, think about how much excitement you'll feel in that moment when you sit down with your cup of green tea. In fact, the anticipation of a reward or relaxation moment can be quite strong. For instance, I've heard people are happier while planning their vacations than when they are actually on them! The psychology behind reward anticipation, or as I call it, "plan-it-yourself excitement," is real![137] Try to think ahead and build in those rewarding moments to find out how much more excitement you can bring to your life.

Figuring out how to revel in the excitement of all that life has to offer is not easily done by everyone. You can build in the ways to find excitement in your life, which you deserve, by trying these tips! Keep working by building in steps like anticipation of rewards and gratitude, which will have you thrilled in no time.

(*The Huffington Post*, May 2017)

5 REASONS TO BE HONEST

Within this competitive world, the advantages of being honest may be unclear to some. When we feel uncertain that honesty will play to our success, it can be tempting to veer from truthfulness. However, there is much more to gain from being honest than we might think.

Here are five reasons to be honest that you may or may not have thought of.

1. HONESTY CLEARS YOUR CONSCIENCE.

Dishonesty forces people to continue to be dishonest in order to avoid telling the truth. A clear conscience can escape people who are habitually dishonest. However, honestly expressing ourselves—in appropriate settings, to those who care and have the time—can help us. We can avoid restraint, pretense, or internal mental conflict. We can live in the present. The clutter that we may have in our thoughts and emotions is cleared. In turn, we are hooked into the present and free our conscience. We can also enjoy better awareness of our present emotions and feel good about ourselves.

2. HONESTY MAKES US BETTER DECISION-MAKERS.

Having a clear conscience can help us be better decision-makers. How so? Being honest helps base decisions on facts, rather than on all the previous times you were dishonest. For example, if you are running for a position on the Parent Teacher Student Association (PTSA) for a local high school, you will make decisions on pressing issues, and you need to base them on the facts of a situation. With an honest approach, you can run with a clearer mind and stay truthful during your time of service, rather than saying what is convenient or what helps your image.

3. HONESTY HELPS US GENERATE AND RECEIVE TRUST.

Most relationships thrive on honesty. The best friendships, familial bonds, and other key relationships are held together with trust. According to relationship expert John Gottman, trust is found to be one of the leading issues among couples.[138] Our ability to depend on our closest social partners and circles makes us feel secure, comforted, and loved. Such essential supportive mechanisms can propel individuals into further success, health and happiness. An honest conversation is more pleasant and intimate, creates a truthful exchange, promotes fulfilling relationships, and provides feelings of tranquility. And as I have explained before, studies show that quality relationships are the number-one predictor of good health and happiness.

4. HONESTY PAVES THE WAY FOR GREATER SUCCESS.

The job market provides a good case for why we should be honest. For example, if we are applying for a new job and need a professional reference, we will need to honestly cite all prior jobs held with contacts who can confirm our employment history. If you are not honest on your resume, you will have a tough time navigating the referencing process. When in doubt, being honest will help you reach greater success, including while applying for a job.

5. HONESTY ENABLES HAPPINESS THROUGH PERSONAL GROWTH.

When we are honest with ourselves, we can reflect accurately, better appreciate our identity i.e., inner qualities, and nurture personal growth. Personal growth, in turn, allows us to quickly find other positive emotions, such as trust, self-esteem and acceptance. These positive emotions can generate greater and more consistent happiness. To provide one example, if we cannot be honest enough to admit we have a bad habit of overeating, we will never pursue exercise or a proper diet. Engaging in a successful diet and exercise routine is an example of personal honesty turned commitment that can lead to happier living.

Feeling good about honesty and its positive consequences? Hope so. Sometimes it might be very difficult to be honest, but remember that having courage now prevents dishonesty from biting back later. Now that you've reviewed the above tips, hopefully you have more reasons to be honest and enjoy a happier and more successful life!

(*The Huffington Post*, March 2017)

ENJOYING LIFE'S SIMPLE TREASURES

Everyday distractions may keep some of us from acknowledging the simple treasures in our lives. Here are a few of life's simple pleasures among many that we cannot take for granted.

1. ENJOYING NATURE

Certainly, we keep to forecasts on our phones or the television to plan our days and weeks ahead, but have you stepped back to notice just how much you enjoy the sunshine on a clear day? The sight of flowers or a freshly minted lawn can quickly lift your spirits. Walks in nature are often so refreshing that we ought to remember how valuable the gift of nature really can be.

2. A SIMPLE HUG

Whether for an outstanding occasion, such as a birthday or graduation, or just because, a hug can show your inner affection and can even touch someone's heart. Give that warm embrace regularly and your affection will find its way back to you.

3. A GOOD NIGHT'S SLEEP

Sleep is so vital to our well-being, yet often we forget how nice it feels to sleep well. A good night's rest is a jewel not to be forsaken. Through any phase in life, receiving good sleep should be valued and pursued as best possible. Many who wrestle to find comfort with their shuteye can attest to the value of sleeping well. Try not to take it for granted.

4. LIFTING SOMEONE'S SPIRITS

The way another person can help lift sadness away from our expression is something we don't soon forget. It is a simple treasure both to receive and to give this spirit-boosting gesture. How noble is it to be able to cheer someone up? Try this and you'll feel happier yourself in no time.

5. A GLASS OF WATER

For those who might fast, or simply don't have access to clean drinking water, the commodity of hydration may be even more valued than by those who are privileged with it consistently. There ought to be unending appreciation for a clean, refreshing glass of water. It is a tremendously significant part of lives—for health and sanitation reasons, among others—and should be valued to the fullest.

The next time you might be overwhelmed or just get a moment, remember these simple treasures in life and how lucky you could be to enjoy these as often as you can.

(*The Huffington Post*, July 2016)

COMPILED QUOTES

"In the face of brokenness, gratitude has the power to heal. In the face of despair, gratitude has the power to bring hope. In other words, gratitude can help us cope with hard times." *–Dr. Robert Emmons*

"Every inhalation of the breath prolongs life and every exhalation of it brings joy to the soul." *–Saadi*

"The deepest craving of human nature is the need to be appreciated." *–Dr. William James*

"Life is not measured by the number of breaths we take, but by the moments that take our breath away." *–Dr. Maya Angelou*

"If one is lucky, a solitary fantasy can totally transform one million realities." *–Dr. Maya Angelou*

"The biggest communication problem is that we do not listen to understand. We listen to reply." *–Dr. Stephen Covey*

"You get in life what you have the courage to ask for." *–Oprah Winfrey*

"If you're always trying to be normal, you will never know how amazing you can be." *–Dr. Maya Angelou*

“Your legacy is every life you’ve touched.” *–Dr. Maya Angelou*

“Nobody’s journey is seamless or smooth. We all stumble. We all have setbacks. It’s just life’s way of saying, ‘Time to change course.’” *–Oprah Winfrey*

“Often it’s the deepest pain which empowers you to grow into your highest self.” *–Karen Salmansohn*

“The meaning of life is to find your gift. The purpose of life is to give it away.” *–Pablo Picasso*

“To thine own self be true.” *–William Shakespeare*

“Create the highest, grandest vision possible for your life, because you become what you believe.” *–Oprah Winfrey*

“Healthy relationships involve sharing both ups and downs. People are more likely to respond positively to you if they sense that you’re truly happy for them.” *–Tai Goodwin*

“The difference between a successful person and others is not a lack of strength, nor a lack of knowledge, but a lack of will.” *–Vince Lombardi*

“Human beings are members of a whole
In creation of one essence and soul
If one member is afflicted with pain
Other members uneasy will remain
If you have no sympathy for human pain
The name of human you cannot retain.” *–Saadi*

The articles in this book were written by the author originally for these publications: *Psychology Today, The Huffington Post, Success Magazine, Entrepreneur Magazine, Mindful.org*, and *GratCircle.com.* Additional research and writing, as well as revisions, are included in this compilation of work.

ENDNOTES

[1] Lyubomirsky, Sonja. "Expressing Gratitude." Gratefulness.org. November 01, 2017. https://gratefulness.org/resource/expressing-gratitude/.

[2] Barker, Eric. "Neuroscience Reveals 4 Rituals That Will Make You Happy." The Week. February 28, 2016. https://theweek.com/articles/601157/neuroscience-reveals-4-rituals-that-make-happy.

[3] Emmons, Robert A., and Michael E. McCullough. "Counting Blessings versus Burdens: An Experimental Investigation of Gratitude and Subjective Well-being in Daily Life." *Journal of Personality and Social Psychology* 84, no. 2 (2003): 377-89. doi:10.1037/0022-3514.84.2.377.

[4] Barker, Eric. "Neuroscience Reveals."

[5] Stevens, Francis L., Robin A. Hurley, and Katherine H. Taber. "Anterior Cingulate Cortex: Unique Role in Cognition and Emotion." *The Journal of Neuropsychiatry and Clinical Neurosciences* 23, no. 2 (April 1, 2011): 121-25. doi:10.1176/jnp.23.2.jnp121.

[6] "Giving Thanks Can Make You Happier." Healthbeat. November 2011. https://www.health.harvard.edu/healthbeat/giving-thanks-can-make-you-happier.

[7] Harvard. T.H. Chan School of Public Health. "Optimism May Reduce Risk of Dying Prematurely among Women." News release, December 07, 2016. Harvard T.H. Chan School of Public Health. https://www.hsph.harvard.edu/news/press-releases/optimism-premature-death-women/.

[8] Conversano, Ciro, Alessandro Rotondo, Elena Lensi, Olivia Della Vista, Francesca Arpone, and Mario Antonio Reda. "Optimism and Its Impact on Mental and Physical Well-Being." *Clinical Practice & Epidemiology in Mental Health* 6 (May 14, 2010): 25-29. doi:10.2174/1745017901006010025.

[9] Lyubomirsky, Sonja. "Eight Ways Gratitude Boosts Happiness." Gratefulness.org. November 01, 2017. https://gratefulness.org/resource/eight-ways/.

[10] Waldinger, Robert. "About Happiness." Robert Waldinger. June 19, 2018. https://robertwaldinger.com/about-happiness/.

[11] Lyubomirsky, Sonja. *The How of Happiness: A Scientific Approach to Getting the Life You Want.* Penguin Press HC, 2007.

[12] Ohio State University. "Gratitude interventions don't help with depression, anxiety: Being grateful has benefits, but not for these issues." ScienceDaily. www.sciencedaily.com/releases/2020/03/200309130010.htm.

[13] Cregg, David R., and Jennifer S. Cheavens. "Gratitude Interventions: Effective Self-help? A Meta-analysis of the Impact on Symptoms of Depression and Anxiety." *Journal of Happiness Studies* 22, no. 1 (February 22, 2020): 413-45. doi:10.1007/s10902-020-00236-6.

[14] Kong, Feng, Jingjing Zhao, Xuqun You, and Yanhui Xiang. "Gratitude and the brain: Trait gratitude mediates the association between structural variations in the medial prefrontal cortex and life satisfaction." Emotion 20, no. 6 (2019): 917-26. doi:10.1037/emo0000617.

[15] Morin, Amy. "7 Scientifically Proven Benefits of Gratitude." Psychology Today. April 03, 2015. https://www.psychologytoday.com/us/blog/what-mentally-strong-people-dont-do/201504/7-scientifically-proven-benefits-gratitude.

[16] Schwartzberg, Louie. TEDxSF. June 2011. https://www.ted.com/talks/louie_schwartzberg_nature_beauty_gratitude.

[17] Froh, Jeffrey J., Giacomo Bono, and Robert Emmons. "Being Grateful Is beyond Good Manners: Gratitude and Motivation to Contribute to Society among Early Adolescents." *Motivation and Emotion* 34, no. 2 (June 1, 2010): 144-57. doi:10.1007/s11031-010-9163-z.

[18] Hopper, Elizabeth, Ph.D. "How Gratitude Helps Us Build Better Relationships." HealthyPsych.com. April 1, 2015. https://healthypsych.com/how-gratitude-helps-us-build-better-relationships/.

[19] Algoe, Sara B., Jonathan Haidt, and Shelly L. Gable. "Beyond Reciprocity: Gratitude and Relationships in Everyday Life." *Emotion* 8, no. 3 (June 2008): 425-29. doi:10.1037/1528-3542.8.3.425.

[20] Waldinger, Robert. "About Happiness." Robert Waldinger. June 19, 2018. https://robertwaldinger.com/about-happiness/.

[21] LaMotte, Sandee. "Five Ways to Improve Your Mental Health in 2020." CNN. January 08, 2020. https://www.cnn.com/2020/01/03/health/mental-health-2020-wellness/index.html.

[22] "Chronic Stress Puts Your Health at Risk." Mayo Clinic. March 19, 2019. https://www.mayoclinic.org/healthy-lifestyle/stress-management/in-depth/stress/art-20046037.

[23] Emmons, Robert A. *The Little Book of Gratitude*. Octopus Books, 2016.

[24] Lau, Bobo Hi-Po, and Cecilia Cheng. "Gratitude and Coping among Familial Caregivers of Persons with Dementia." *Aging & Mental Health* 21, no. 4 (November 27, 2015): 445-53. doi:10.1080/13607863.2015.1114588.

[25] Kwon, Hyukwoo, and Yongrae Cho. "Effects of Gratitude Intervention on Job-Seeking Stress and Mental Health Variables and Meaning in Life as Its Mediator." *Korean Journal of Clinical Psychology* 38, no. 2 (2019): 182-98. doi:10.15842/kjcp.2019.38.2.005.

[26] Lee, Mary Katherine A. "Gratitude as an Antidote to Anxiety and Depression: All the Benefits, None of the Side Effects." Lerner Center for Public Health Promotion. May 28, 2019. https://lernercenter.syr.edu/2019/05/28/lerner-center-program-coordinator-mary-kate-lee-publishes-issue-brief-on-gratitude/.

[27] Tye, Kristine, MA, LMFT. "7 Ways Anxiety Actually Works to Your Advantage." GoodTherapy.org Therapy Blog. February 2, 2016. https://www.goodtherapy.org/blog/7-ways-anxiety-actually-works-to-your-advantage-0202165.

[28] "Anxiety Disorders." Mayo Clinic. May 04, 2018. https://www.mayoclinic.org/diseases-conditions/anxiety/symptoms-causes/syc-20350961.

[29] *Ibid.*

[30] Petrocchi, Nicola, and Alessandro Couyoumdjian. "The Impact of Gratitude on Depression and Anxiety: The Mediating Role of Criticizing, Attacking, and Reassuring the Self." *Self and Identity* 15, no. 2 (October 13, 2015): 191-205. doi:10.1080/15298868.2015.1095794.

[31] Heckendorf, Hanna, Dirk Lehr, David Daniel Ebert, and Henning Freund. "Efficacy of an Internet and App-based Gratitude Intervention in Reducing Repetitive Negative Thinking and Mechanisms of Change in the Interventions Effect on Anxiety and Depression: Results from a Randomized Controlled Trial." *Behaviour Research and Therapy* 119 (June 8, 2019). doi:10.1016/j.brat.2019.103415.

[32] Marchant, Natalie L., Lise R. Lovland, Rebecca Jones, Alexa Pichet Binette, Julie Gonneaud, Eider M. Arenaza-Urquijo, Gael Chételat, and Sylvia Villeneuve. "Repetitive Negative Thinking Is Associated with Amyloid, Tau, and Cognitive Decline." *Alzheimers & Dementia* 16, no. 7 (January 14, 2020): 1054-064. doi:10.1002/alz.12116.

[33] Cripps, Danielle. *Exploring the Effectiveness of a School-based Gratitude Intervention on Childrens Levels of Anxiety, Sense of School Belonging and Sleep Quality*. Master's thesis, University of Southampton, 2019. University of Southampton Institutional Repository, 2019.

[34] Cregg, David R., and Jennifer S. Cheavens. "Gratitude Interventions: Effective Self-help? A Meta-analysis of the Impact on Symptoms of Depression and Anxiety." *Journal of Happiness Studies* 22 (January 2021): 1-33. doi:10.1007/s10902-020-00236-6.

[35] Wood, Alex M., John Maltby, Raphael Gillett, P. Alex Linley, and Stephen Joseph. "The Role of Gratitude in the Development of Social Support, Stress, and Depression: Two Longitudinal Studies." *Journal of Research in Personality* 42, no. 4 (August 2008): 854-71. doi:10.1016/j.jrp.2007.11.003.

[36] Emmons, Robert. "How Gratitude Can Help You Through Hard Times." Greater Good Magazine. May 13, 2013. https://greatergood.berkeley.edu/article/item/how_gratitude_can_help_you_through_hard_times.

[37] Voci, Alberto, Chiara A. Veneziani, and Giulia Fuochi. "Relating Mindfulness, Heartfulness, and Psychological Well-Being: The Role of Self-Compassion and Gratitude." *Mindfulness* 10, no. 2 (June 19, 2018): 339-51. doi:10.1007/s12671-018-0978-0.

[38] Jans-Beken, Lilian, Nele Jacobs, Mayke Janssens, Sanne Peeters, Jennifer Reijnders, Lilian Lechner, and Johan Lataster. "Gratitude and Health: An Updated Review." *The Journal of Positive Psychology* 15, no. 6 (August 06, 2019): 743-82. doi:10.1080/17439760.2019.1651888.

[39] Emmons, Robert A., and Robin Stern. "Gratitude as a Psychotherapeutic Intervention." *Journal of Clinical Psychology* 69, no. 8 (June 17, 2013): 846-55. doi:10.1002/jclp.22020.

[40] Glasgow, Kimberly, Jessika Vitak, Yla Tausczik, and Clay Fink. ""With Your Help... We Begin to Heal": Social Media Expressions of Gratitude in the Aftermath of Disaster." *Social, Cultural, and Behavioral Modeling Lecture Notes in Computer Science* 9708 (June 6, 2016): 226-36. doi:10.1007/978-3-319-39931-7_22.

[41] Sztachańska, Joanna, Izabela Krejtz, and John B. Nezlek. "Using a Gratitude Intervention to Improve the Lives of Women With Breast Cancer: A Daily Diary Study." *Frontiers in Psychology* 10 (June 12, 2019). doi:10.3389/fpsyg.2019.01365.

[42] Kyeong, Sunghyon, Joohan Kim, Dae Jin Kim, Hesun Erin Kim, and Jae-Jin Kim. "Effects of Gratitude Meditation on Neural Network Functional Connectivity and Brain-heart Coupling." *Scientific Reports* 7, no. 1 (July 11, 2017). doi:10.1038/s41598-017-05520-9.

[43] "Nucleus Accumbens: Location, Structure, Functions & Cells." The Human Memory. November 25, 2020. https://human-memory.net/nucleus-accumbens/.

[44] Marsh, Abigail A. "The Neuroscience of Empathy." *Current Opinion in Behavioral Sciences* 19 (February 2018): 110-15. doi:10.1016/j.cobeha.2017.12.016.

[45] *Ibid.*

[46] Kong, Feng, Jingjing Zhao, Xuqun You, and Yanhui Xiang. "Gratitude and the brain: Trait gratitude mediates the association between structural variations in the medial prefrontal cortex and life satisfaction." *Emotion* 20, no. 6 (2019): 917-26. doi:10.1037/emo0000617.

[47] Smith, Jeremy Adam, Kira M. Newman, Jason Marsh, and Dacher Keltner. *The Gratitude Project: How the Science of Thankfulness Can Rewire Our Brains for Resilience, Optimism, and the Greater Good.* New Harbinger Publishing, 2021.

[48] Chun, Sanghee, and Youngkhill Lee. ""I Am Just Thankful": The Experience of Gratitude following Traumatic Spinal Cord Injury." *Disability and Rehabilitation* 35, no. 1 (May 27, 2012): 11-19. doi:10.3109/09638288.2012.687026.

[49] Jordan, Hamilton. *No Such Thing as a Bad Day: A Memoir*. Thorndike Press, 2001.

[50] Whyte, Steve. "Breathe." Medium. February 11, 2017. https://medium.com/thrive-global/breathe-5749aeb9f4f0.

[51] Lyubomirsky, Sonja. "Expressing Gratitude."

[52] Barker, Eric. "Neuroscience Reveals."

[53] Emmons, Robert A., and Michael E. McCullough. "Counting Blessings."

[54] "Gratitude Journal (Greater Good in Action)." Greater Good in Action - Science-based Practices for a Meaningful Life. https://ggia.berkeley.edu/practice/gratitude_journal.

[55] Miller, Janet. "8 Ways To Have More Gratitude Every Day." Forbes. July 8, 2016. https://www.forbes.com/sites/womensmedia/2016/07/08/8-ways-to-have-more-gratitude-every-day/?sh=5a28369f1d54.

[56] Klibert, Jeffrey, Haresh Rochani, Hani Samawi, Kayla Leleux-Labarge, and Rebecca Ryan. "The Impact of an Integrated Gratitude Intervention on Positive Affect and Coping Resources." *International Journal of Applied Positive Psychology* 3, no. 1-3 (April 16, 2019): 23-41. doi:10.1007/s41042-019-00015-6.

[57] Watkins, Philip C., Robert A. Emmons, Madeline R. Greaves, and Joshua Bell. "Joy Is a Distinct Positive Emotion: Assessment of Joy and Relationship to Gratitude and Well-being." *The Journal of Positive Psychology* 13, no. 5 (December 2017): 522-39. doi:10.1080/17439760.2017.1414298.

[58] "Europe Discusses How to Deal with Pandemic Fatigue." World Health Organization. October 07, 2020. https://www.who.int/news-room/feature-stories/detail/who-europe-discusses-how-to-deal-with-pandemic-fatigue.

[59] Emmons, Robert. "How Gratitude Can Help You Through Hard Times." Greater Good Magazine. May 13, 2013. https://greatergood.berkeley.edu/article/item/how_gratitude_can_help_you_through_hard_times.

[60] "A Quote from Saadi." Goodreads. https://www.goodreads.com/quotes/1274345-human-beings-are-members-of-a-whole-in-creation-of.

[61] Bono, Giacomo, and Jason T. Sender. "How Gratitude Connects Humans to the Best in Themselves and in Others." *Research in Human Development* 15, no. 2 (2018): 1-14. doi:10.1080/15427609.2018.1499350.

[62] Wood, Alex M., Stephen Joseph, and P. Alex Linley. "Coping Style as a Psychological Resource of Grateful People." *Journal of Social and Clinical Psychology* 26, no. 9 (November 2007): 1076-093. doi:10.1521/jscp.2007.26.9.1076.

[63] Greene, Nathan Ritvo, and Katie McGovern. "Gratitude, Psychological Well-being, and Perceptions of Posttraumatic Growth in Adults Who Lost a Parent in Childhood." *Death Studies* 41, no. 7 (February 2017). doi:10.1080/07481187.2017.1296505.

[64] Wilson, Jane Taylor. "Brightening the Mind: The Impact of Practicing Gratitude on Focus and Resilience in Learning." *Journal of the Scholarship of Teaching and Learning* 16, no. 4 (August 2016): 1-13. doi:10.14434/josotl.v16i4.19998.

[65] Zhang, Wendy, Nadia O'Brien, Jamie I. Forrest, Kate A. Salters, Thomas L. Patterson, Julio S. G. Montaner, Robert S. Hogg, and Viviane D. Lima. "Validating a Shortened Depression Scale (10 Item CES-D) among HIV-Positive People in British Columbia, Canada." *PLoS ONE*, July 19, 2012. doi:10.1371/journal.pone.0040793.

[66] Petrocchi, Nicola, and Alessandro Couyoumdjian. "The Impact of Gratitude on Depression and Anxiety: The Mediating Role of Criticizing, Attacking, and Reassuring the Self." *Self and Identity* 15, no. 2 (October 13, 2015): 191-205. doi:10.1080/15298868.2015.1095794.

[67] Montesano, Adrián, Guillem Feixas, Franz Caspar, and David Winter. "Depression and Identity: Are Self-Constructions Negative or Conflictual?" *Frontiers in Psychology* 8 (May 30, 2017). doi:10.3389/fpsyg.2017.00877.

[68] Liang, Hongyu, Chen Chen, Fang Li, Shuman Wu, Lixin Wang, Xue Zheng, and Benjun Zeng. "Mediating Effects of Peace of Mind and Rumination on the Relationship between Gratitude and Depression among Chinese University Students." *Current Psychology* 39, no. 4 (April 14, 2018): 1430-437. doi:10.1007/s12144-018-9847-1.

[69] Røgild-Müller, Laura, and Julie Robinson. "Emergence and Experience of "Peace of Mind": What Can Classic Writers Tell Us?" *Human Arenas*, November 04, 2020. doi:10.1007/s42087-020-00147-1.

[70] Sirois, Fuschia M., and Alex M. Wood. "Gratitude Uniquely Predicts Lower Depression in Chronic Illness Populations: A Longitudinal Study of Inflammatory Bowel Disease and Arthritis." *Health Psychology* 36, no. 2 (2017): 122-32. doi:10.1037/hea0000436.

[71] Khorrami, Najma, M.P.H. "Gratitude Helps Minimize Feelings of Stress." Psychology Today. July 07, 2020. https://www.psychologytoday.com/us/blog/comfort-gratitude/202007/gratitude-helps-minimize-feelings-stress.

[72] Khorrami, Najma, M.P.H. "Gratitude Helps Curb Anxiety." Psychology Today. July 20, 2020. https://www.psychologytoday.com/us/blog/comfort-gratitude/202007/gratitude-helps-curb-anxiety.

[73] Khorrami, Najma, M.P.H. "Gratitude Protects Against Depression." Psychology Today. December 11, 2020. https://www.psychologytoday.com/us/blog/comfort-gratitude/202012/gratitude-protects-against-depression.

[74] Khorrami, Najma, M.P.H. "Why Expressing Gratitude Strengthens Our Relationships." Psychology Today. June 24, 2020. https://www.psychologytoday.com/us/blog/comfort-gratitude/202006/why-expressing-gratitude-strengthens-our-relationships.

[75] Bono, Giacomo, Susan Mangan, Michael Fauteux, and Jason Sender. "A New Approach to Gratitude Interventions in High Schools That Supports Student Wellbeing." *The Journal of Positive Psychology* 15, no. 2 (July 2020): 1-9. doi:10.1080/17439760.2020.1789712.

[76] Kong, Feng, Jingjing Zhao, Xuqun You, and Yanhui Xiang. "Gratitude and the Brain: Trait Gratitude Mediates the Association between Structural Variations in the Medial Prefrontal Cortex and Life Satisfaction." *Emotion* 20, no. 6 (June 2019). doi:10.1037/emo0000617.

[77] Barker, Eric. "Neuroscience Reveals 4 Rituals That Will Make You Happy." The Week. February 28, 2016. https://theweek.com/articles/601157/neuroscience-reveals-4-rituals-that-make-happy.

[78] Emmons, Robert A., and Michael E. Mccullough. "Counting Blessings versus Burdens: An Experimental Investigation of Gratitude and Subjective Well-being in Daily Life." *Journal of Personality and Social Psychology* 84, no. 2 (2003): 377-89. doi:10.1037/0022-3514.84.2.377.

[79] "Teens and Social Media Use: What's the Impact?" Mayo Clinic. December 21, 2019. https://www.mayoclinic.org/healthy-lifestyle/tween-and-teen-health/in-depth/teens-and-social-media-use/art-20474437.

[80] Bono, Giacomo, Susan Mangan, Michael Fauteux, and Jason Sender. "A New Approach."

[81] Littlefield, Christopher. "Use Gratitude to Counter Stress and Uncertainty." Harvard Business Review. October 20, 2020. https://hbr.org/2020/10/use-gratitude-to-counter-stress-and-uncertainty.

[82] Wong, Joel, and Joshua Brown. "How Gratitude Changes You and Your Brain." Mindful. June 28, 2017. https://www.mindful.org/gratitude-changes-brain/.

[83] Domet, Stephanie. "A Simple Mindful Gratitude Exercise." Mindful. November 13, 2018. https://www.mindful.org/a-simple-mindful-gratitude-exercise/.

[84] Hendriksen, Ellen. "How Not to Care What Other People Think." Scientific American. April 07, 2016. https://www.scientificamerican.com/article/how-not-to-care-what-other-people-think/.

[85] Molloy, Parker. "Michelle Obama Sat down with Oprah for an Important Chat about Criticism." Upworthy. December 20, 2016. https://www.upworthy.com/michelle-obama-sat-down-with-oprah-for-an-important-chat-about-criticism.

[86] Raghunathan, Raj. "How Not to Worry About What Others Think of You." Psychology Today. March 03, 2016. https://www.psychologytoday.com/us/blog/sapient-nature/201603/how-not-worry-about-what-others-think-you.

[87] Hutson, Matthew. "Beyond Happiness: The Upside of Feeling Down." Psychology Today. January 6, 2015. https://www.psychologytoday.com/intl/articles/201501/beyond-happiness-the-upside-feeling-down.

[88] Goalcast. June 12, 2017. https://www.goalcast.com/2017/06/12/oprah-winfrey-whats-your-legacy/.

[89] Vitelli, Romeo, Ph.D. "Can Lifelong Learning Help As We Age?" Psychology Today. October 14, 2012. https://www.psychologytoday.com/us/blog/media-spotlight/201210/can-lifelong-learning-help-we-age.

[90] Ford, Mark Morgan. "Good Manners And Success." Early To Rise. September 05, 2001. https://www.earlytorise.com/good-manners-and-success/.

[91] *First Lady Michelle Obama and Oprah Winfrey Hold a Conversation on the Next Generation of Women*. Performed by Michelle Obama and Oprah Winfrey. YouTube. June 14, 2016. https://www.youtube.com/watch?app=desktop&v=LCmwkjSzr2g.

[92] Harvard. T.H. Chan School of Public Health. "Optimism May Reduce Risk of Dying Prematurely among Women." News release, December 07, 2016. Harvard T.H. Chan School of Public Health. https://www.hsph.harvard.edu/news/press-releases/optimism-premature-death-women/.

[93] Harvard. T.H. Chan School of Public Health. "Optimism May Reduce Risk of Dying Prematurely among Women." News release, December 07, 2016. Harvard T.H. Chan School of Public Health. https://www.hsph.harvard.edu/news/press-releases/optimism-premature-death-women/.

[94] "Benefits of Exercise." MedlinePlus. https://medlineplus.gov/benefitsofexercise.html.

[95] Olaniyan, Ayo. "50 Ways To Build Your Optimism." Steven Aitchison. https://www.stevenaitchison.co.uk/50-ways-to-build-your-optimism/.

[96] Bradberry, Travis. "What Successful People (Who Are Actually Happy) Do Differently." HuffPost. January 15, 2017. https://www.huffpost.com/entry/what-successful-people-wh_b_14137794?section=us_healthy-living.

[97] Mitchell, Kevin. "Roger Federer Continues to Defy Time and Critics with Indian Wells Win." The Guardian. March 19, 2017. https://www.theguardian.com/sport/2017/mar/19/roger-federer-defy-time-critics-win-indian-wells.

[98] Hodgkinson, Mark. "Roger Federer's Team Are the Secret to His Success." British GQ. June 25, 2018. https://www.gq-magazine.co.uk/article/roger-federers-team-are-the-secret-of-his-success.

[99] Adams, R.L. "50 Profitable Side Hustle Ideas." Entrepreneur. https://www.entrepreneur.com/article/293954.

[100] Waldinger, Robert. "About Happiness." Robert Waldinger. June 19, 2018. https://robertwaldinger.com/about-happiness/.

[101] *Ibid.*

[102] Jimenez, Jesus. "6 Ways to Be More Optimistic." SUCCESS. September 16, 2016. https://www.success.com/top-of-mind-6-ways-to-be-more-optimistic/.

[103] Harvard. T.H. Chan School of Public Health. "Optimism May Reduce Risk of Dying Prematurely among Women." News release, December 07, 2016. Harvard T.H. Chan School of Public Health. https://www.hsph.harvard.edu/news/press-releases/optimism-premature-death-women/.

[104] Rizzo, Steve. "Why It's All About Attitude." SUCCESS. January 25, 2017. https://www.success.com/why-its-all-about-attitude/.

[105] Bradberry, Travis. "How Positivity Makes You Healthy and Successful." SUCCESS. March 13, 2017. https://www.success.com/how-positivity-makes-you-healthy-and-successful/.

[106] Harvard. T.H. Chan School of Public Health. "Optimism May."

[107] Park, Nansook, Christopher Peterson, Daniel Szvarca, Randy J. Vander Molen, Eric S. Kim, and Kevin Collon. "Positive Psychology and Physical Health." *American Journal of Lifestyle Medicine* 10, no. 3 (September 26, 2014): 200-06. doi:10.1177/1559827614550277.

[108] Power, Rhett. "7 Ways to Lead a More Satisfying Life." SUCCESS. January 11, 2017. https://www.success.com/7-ways-to-lead-a-more-satisfying-life/.

[109] Robbins, Mel. "How to Build Your Courage to Achieve Anything." SUCCESS. October 31, 2016. https://www.success.com/how-to-build-your-courage-to-achieve-anything/.

[110] Goodwin, Tai. "Stop Hating: Five Reasons It Pays to Get Happy About Other People's Success." HuffPost. January 23, 2014. https://www.huffpost.com/entry/happiness-success_b_4266245.

[111] Hardy, Benjamin P. "34 Undeniable Truths About Becoming Successful." SUCCESS. March 29, 2017. https://www.success.com/34-things-you-need-to-know-about-becoming-successful/.

[112] Harpham, Bruce. "The Best Career Advice, From Successful People Who Made It to the Top." SUCCESS. June 30, 2016. https://www.success.com/the-best-career-advice-from-successful-people-who-made-it-to-the-top/.

[113] Bilyeu, Tom. "Ask These Questions to Reframe Your Perspective on Life." SUCCESS. December 19, 2016. https://www.success.com/ask-these-questions-to-reframe-your-perspective-on-life/.

[114] Jimenez, Jesus. "How to Strengthen Your Willpower." SUCCESS. September 7, 2016. https://www.success.com/top-of-mind-how-to-strengthen-your-willpower/.

[115] Imafidon, Casey. "10 Little Things Successful People Do Differently." SUCCESS. July 19, 2016. https://www.success.com/10-little-things-successful-people-do-differently/.

[116] Rollin, Jennifer, MSW, LCSW-C. "4 Quick Mindfulness Practices For Coping With Anxiety." HuffPost. August 18, 2016. https://www.huffpost.com/entry/4-quick-mindfulness-practices-for-coping-with-anxiety_b_57b625c0e4b029a9a46516b6.

[117] Hayes, Steven C., Ph.D. "From Loss to Love." Psychology Today. June 18, 2018. https://www.psychologytoday.com/us/articles/201806/loss-love.

[118] "How to Let Go of Someone, 6 Tips to Move Forward." Tony Robbins. https://www.tonyrobbins.com/mind-meaning/the-power-of-letting-go/.

[119] "Our Intentional Activities Are The Key to Happiness." Emotional Affair Journey. https://www.emotionalaffair.org/our-intentional-activities-are-the-key-to-happiness/.

[120] Ross, Jennifer. "Roko Belic Talks Happy Documentary." July 07, 2010. https://www.pastemagazine.com/movies/roko-belic/roko-belic-talks-documentary-on-happiness/.

[121] "Our Intentional Activities." Emotional Affair Journey.

[122] Lyubomirsky, Sonja. *The How of Happiness: A Scientific Approach to Getting the Life You Want.* Penguin Press HC, 2007.

[123] Becker, Anne E., M.D., Ph.D., and Arthur Kleinman, Ph.D. "Mental Health and the Global Agenda: NEJM." New England Journal of Medicine. July 4, 2013. https://www.nejm.org/doi/full/10.1056/NEJMra1110827#t=article.

[124] Collins, Pamela Y., Vikram Patel, Sarah S. Joestl, Dana March, Thomas R. Insel, Abdallah S. Daar, Isabel A. Bordin, E. Jane Costello, Maureen Durkin, Christopher Fairburn, Roger I. Glass, Wayne Hall, Yueqin Huang, Steven E. Hyman, Kay Jamison, Sylvia Kaaya, Shitij Kapur, Arthur Kleinman, Adesola Ogunniyi, Angel Otero-Ojeda, Mu-Ming Poo, Vijayalakshmi Ravindranath, Barbara J. Sahakian, Shekhar Saxena, Peter A. Singer, Dan J. Stein, Warwick Anderson, Muhammad A. Dhansay, Wendy Ewart, Anthony Phillips, Susan Shurin, and Mark Walport. "Grand Challenges in Global Mental Health." *Nature* 475, no. 7354 (July 6, 2011): 27-30. doi:10.1038/475027a.

[125] "Goal 3." United Nations | Department of Economic and Social Affairs. https://sdgs.un.org/goals/goal3.

[126] O'Donnell, Kelly, PsyD. "Global Mental Health: Strategies for Staying Current." American Psychological Association. March 2014. https://www.apa.org/international/pi/2014/03/global-health.

[127] D'Souza, Joy. "Will, Kate And Harry Launch New Campaign To End Mental Health Stigma." HuffPost Canada. April 25, 2016. https://www.huffingtonpost.ca/2016/04/25/mental-health-stigma_n_9774338.html.

[128] Holmes, Lindsay, and Abigail Williams. "13 Times Celebrities Got Real About Mental Health." HuffPost. October 10, 2015. https://www.huffpost.com/entry/celebrity-mental-illness-quotes_n_5617e500e4b0dbb8000e37d7.

[129] D'Souza, Joy. "Will, Kate And Harry."

[130] McCoy, William. "Does Stretching Release Endorphins?" The Nest. https://woman.thenest.com/stretching-release-endorphins-20877.html.

[131] Broderick, Evelyn. "Seratonin Endorphins & Exercise." Healthfully. August 14, 2017. https://healthfully.com/197569-seratonin-endorphins-exercise.html.

[132] "Exploring The Link Between Exercise And Happiness." HuffPost UK. August 22, 2016. https://www.huffingtonpost.co.uk/entry/the-link-between-exercise-and-happiness_uk_573d97bae4b058ab71e656f3.

[133] Benwell, Wendy, PT, DPT, MS. "How to Listen to Your Body to Avoid Injury." ACTIVE.com. https://www.active.com/triathlon/articles/how-to-listen-to-your-body-to-avoid-injury.

[134] "Personal Goal Setting: Planning to Live Your Life Your Way." MindTools. https://www.mindtools.com/page6.html.

[135] Brooks, Arthur C. "Choose to Be Grateful. It Will Make You Happier." The New York Times. November 21, 2015. https://www.nytimes.com/2015/11/22/opinion/sunday/choose-to-be-grateful-it-will-make-you-happier.html?_r=0.

[136] Lyubomirsky, Sonja. "Expressing Gratitude." Gratefulness.org. November 01, 2017. https://gratefulness.org/resource/expressing-gratitude/.

[137] Nawijn, Jeroen, Miquelle A. Marchand, Ruut Veenhoven, and Ad J. Vingerhoets. "Vacationers Happier, but Most Not Happier After a Holiday." *Applied Research in Quality of Life* 5 (February 10, 2010): 35-47. doi:10.1007/s11482-009-9091-9.

[138] Firestone, Lisa, Ph.D. "5 Ways to Build Trust and Honesty in Your Relationship." Psychology Today. June 29, 2015. https://www.psychologytoday.com/us/blog/compassion-matters/201506/5-ways-build-trust-and-honesty-in-your-relationship.

ABOUT THE AUTHOR

Najma Khorrami founded her social media app-based company, Gratitude Circle, in 2017. She grew up in Northern Virginia, outside of Washington, D.C. She attended The George Washington University and earned a master's degree in public health in 2012. Her background in public health led her to pursue and obtain a Certificate in Global Health from the Johns Hopkins Bloomberg School of Public Health. In her time as a public health professional, she worked for The Center for Global Health Diplomacy. She has been published in the *International Journal of Gynecology and Obstetrics* and the *Journal of Perinatology*. She is also the author of a children's book, *Self-Care with Ted and Friends*. Her work, including the articles in this book, has been published in publications including *The Huffington Post*, *Psychology Today*, and others.